JAVA PROGRAMMING FOR BEGINNERS

TOP PRIMARY PROGRAMMING LANGUAGE FOR DEVELOPERS AT TOP COMPANIES. A PRACTICAL GUIDE YOU CAN'T MISS TO LEARN JAVA IN 7 DAYS OR LESS, WITH HANDS-ON PROJECTS.

ERICK THOMPSON

Copyright - 2020 -

All rights reserved.

The content contained within this book may not be reproduced, duplicated or transmitted without direct written permission from the author or the publisher.

Under no circumstances will any blame or legal responsibility be held against the publisher, or author, for any damages, reparation, or monetary loss due to the information contained within this book. Either directly or indirectly.

Legal Notice:

This book is copyright protected. This book is only for personal use. You cannot amend, distribute, sell, use, quote or paraphrase any part, or the content within this book, without the consent of the author or publisher.

Disclaimer Notice:

Please note the information contained within this document is for educational and entertainment purposes only. All effort has been executed to present accurate, up to date, and reliable, complete information. No warranties of any kind are declared or implied. Readers acknowledge that the author is not engaging in the rendering of legal, financial, medical or professional advice. The content within this book has been derived from various sources. Please consult a licensed professional before attempting any techniques outlined in this book.

By reading this document, the reader agrees that under no circumstances is the author responsible for any losses, direct or indirect, which are incurred as a result of the use of information contained within this document, including, but not limited to, - errors, omissions, or inaccuracies.

TABLE OF CONTENTS

INTRODUCTION   6

CHAPTER - 1
    JAVA INTRODUCTION   10

CHAPTER - 2
    GET READY FOR JAVA   21

CHAPTER - 3
    GETTING READY FOR JAVA   31

CHAPTER - 4
    VARIABLES AND OPERATORS   43

CHAPTER - 5
    ARRAYS AND STRING   61

CHAPTER - 6
    PROGRAMMING CONTROL STATEMENT   73

CHAPTER - 7
    ITERATION STATEMENTS AND
    LOOPING STATEMENTS IN JAVA   79

CHAPTER - 8
    CLASSES, OBJECT AND METHODS   88

CHAPTER - 9
    ADVANCED OBJECT
    ORIENTED PROGRAMMING   99

CHAPTER - 10
    COLLECTIONS   116

CHAPTER - 11
    FILE HANDLING   144

CHAPTER - 12
    ADVANCED JAVA   150

CHAPTER - 13
    MODULES   162

CHAPTER - 14
    PROJECTS   172

CONCLUSION   190

INTRODUCTION

Java is one of the most popular programming languages today. For one thing, it is the programming language preferred by almost everyone when it comes to Android programming. Do you want to learn how to develop applications for your smartphone? Learn to program in this language!

Java is widely used to develop secure and powerful web applications, mobile applications, corporate applications, and desktop applications.

This is for people who have absolutely no idea about programming. You will learn programming concepts and nuances that start with the basics while getting the details of Java programming.

Now, isn't Java complicated?

Now that's an interesting question. Well, doesn't all kinds of programming seem complicated from the start? The same goes for Java. Things will clear up pretty quickly once you understand the basics that will be your building blocks for later things that you include in the applications and programs you create.

Java actually offers you some benefits that go beyond other current programming languages.

1. It is the only programming language most used today.

In other words, it is the de facto model. In today's highly connected world, Java is the language code that operates and resides on more than 3 billion devices, according to Oracle.

Java is also consistently the most popular month-to-month programming language, according to the TIOBE Programming Community Index. And why is it a constant favorite among many developers today?

One of the reasons given for its popularity is the large number of real-world applications. Plus, because it's so popular, you'll find plenty of FREE support from a global Java programming community. In case you get stuck while typing your password, you can find a lot of help online.

2. It is a very good precursor for those who want to learn to code.

Some people may suggest C, C #, or another programming language to help beginner beginners learn to write code. But guess that. Java is at the same level. In fact, at some point in the programming process, Java outperforms other programming languages.

Java is a basic programming language: it is different from JavaScript (we will see later). You can program Java code for environments as well as for offline environments. It is a programming language that works on all operating systems. In addition, it is also a programming language that works on all kinds of devices.

3. It makes you think like a programmer.

The nuances of Java programming will make you see and think things like a professional programmer. You will surely learn the different concepts and structures of this programming language, but in the process you will also learn the basics of code writing.

In addition to this, you will also learn Object Oriented Programming (or OOP for short). To truly master OOP, you need to move a little further than good traditional design programming. Through Java, you will learn to see things in both abstract and concrete design that will provide you with a good foundation at this level of programming logic.

4. Java is a professional of all time.

Java has been around for over 2 decades. Now, you may ask, how in the world will this help. Well, that means that every problem you face or the question that comes to mind already has an answer. There are no surprises that someone out there has not yet corrected.

On top of that, learning to program in Java will pave the way for you to create openings in many developer tasks that are definitely very efficient. This is a great language for beginners to start learning how to code.

We will get through all of this and beyond, as we discuss the basics of Java programming for absolute beginners.

CHAPTER - 1

JAVA INTRODUCTION

History of Java

The Java language was structured by James Gosling and first showed up on the scene in May of 1995. The programming language has experienced different discharges, with the current rendition being variant 8.

In the year 2006, Java had discharged the Java Virtual Machine. The Java Virtual Machine is utilized to run Java programs on the pertinent working frameworks, and was made accessible under free programming/open-source dispersion terms.

Beneath we broadly expound on the different forms of Java and the highlights which were presented with every rendition.

JDK 1.1 - Support for the accompanying:

- A broad retooling of the AWT occasion model.
- Inner classes added to the language.
- JavaBeans.
- JDBC.
- RMI.
- Reflection, which bolsters Introspection as it were. No change at runtime is conceivable.
- JIT (Just In Time) compiler on Microsoft Windows stages, delivered for JavaSoft by Symantec.
- Internationalization and Unicode support beginning from Taligent.
- J2SE 1.2 - Support for the accompanying:
- Strictfp catchphrase.
- The Swing graphical API was incorporated into the center classes.
- Sun's JVM was furnished with a JIT compiler.
- Java module.
- Java IDL, an IDL execution for CORBA interoperability.

- Collections structure.
- J2SE 1.3 - Support for the accompanying:
- HotSpot JVM included.
- RMI was altered to help discretionary similarity with CORBA.
- Java Naming and Directory Interface (JNDI) remembered for center libraries.
- Java Platform Debugger Architecture (JPDA).
- JavaSound.
- Synthetic intermediary classes.
- J2SE 1.4 - Support for the accompanying:
- Regular articulations displayed after Perl normal articulations.
- Exception anchoring, which considers a special case to exemplify unique lower-level exemptions.
- Internet Protocol rendition 6 (IPv6) support.
- Non-blocking IO.
- Logging API.
- Image I/O API for perusing and composing pictures in positions like JPEG and PNG.
- Java Web Start included.
- Preferences API (java.util.prefs).
- J2SE 5.0 - Support for the accompanying:
- Generics, which gives arrange time (static) type wellbeing for assortments and takes out the requirement for most pigeonholes.

- Metadata, which is likewise called comments. This permits language builds, for example, classes and strategies to be labeled with extra information, which would then be able to be prepared by metadata-mindful utilities.
- Autoboxing/unpacking. This takes into account programmed transformations between crude kinds, (for example, int) and crude covering classes, (for example, Integer).
- Enumerations. Here the enum watchword makes a typesafe, requested rundown of qualities.
- Varargs. This is the last boundary of a technique, which would now be able to be announced utilizing a sort name followed by three specks.
- Enhanced 'for each' circle. The 'for' circle grammar is reached out with unique punctuation for repeating over every individual from either an exhibit or an Iterable, for example, the standard Collection classes.
- Improved semantics of execution for multi-strung Java programs. The new Java memory model tends to issues of multifaceted nature, adequacy, and execution of past determinations.
- Static imports.
- Java SE 6-Support for the accompanying:

- Scripting Language Support. A nonexclusive API is presented for tight joining with scripting dialects, and implicit Mozilla JavaScript Rhino coordination.
- Dramatic execution enhancements for the center stage and Swing.
- JDBC 4.0 help.
- Support for pluggable comments.
- Many GUI enhancements, for example, mix of SwingWorker in the API, table arranging and sifting, and genuine Swing twofold buffering.
- JVM enhancements, which included synchronization and compiler execution advancements, new calculations and moves up to existing trash assortment calculations, and application fire up execution.
- Java SE 7 - Support for the accompanying:
- JVM support for dynamic dialects, with the new invokedynamic bytecode.
- Compressed 64-piece pointers.
- Strings in the switch articulation.
- Automatic asset the board in the attempt articulation.
- Improved type derivation for conventional case creation.
- Simplified varargs strategy statement.
- Binary whole number literals.
- Allowing underscores in numeric literals.

- Catching various special case types and rethrowing exemptions with improved kind checking.
- New record I/O library. Here help was included for numerous record frameworks, document metadata and emblematic connections.
- Library-level help for elliptic bend cryptography calculations.
- An XRender pipeline for Java 2D, which improves the treatment of highlights explicit to present day GPUs.
- Enhanced library-level help for new system conventions, including SCTP and Sockets Direct Protocol.
- Upstream updates to XML and Unicode.

What is Java?

Java is a programming language that is worked by Sun Microsystems, which was later taken over by the Oracle Corporation. It is intended to run on any working framework that bolsters Java. This is the thing that made the language so well known, in light of the fact that the engineer simply needed to compose the program once, and the program could then sudden spike in demand for any working framework without the requirement for the software engineer to change the code.

A large portion of the advanced applications worked the world over are produced using the Java programming language. A large portion of the server side and business rationale parts of significant applications are based on the Java programming language.

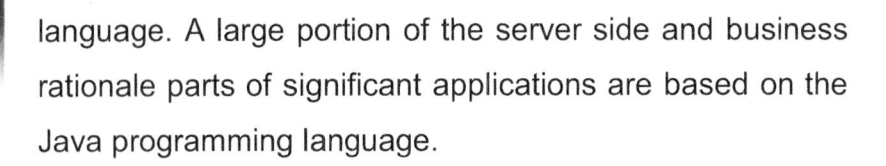

An example Java program is demonstrated as follows.

Model 1: The accompanying system is utilized to feature a basic Java program.

open class HelloWorld

```
{
open static void main(String[] args) {
System.out.println("Hello World!");
}
}
```

During the whole course, you will figure out how to compose projects, for example, the one above, and furthermore learn propelled ideas that will empower you to begin composing total application programs.

A portion of the plan objectives for Java are referenced beneath:

- The language is planned to be composed once and be able to be run on any working framework.

- The language ought to offer help for various programming designing standards.
- The language is proposed to be utilized in creating programming segments reasonable for arrangement in circulated conditions.
- Portability is a significant factor. This is the reason Java can run on Windows, Linux and the MacOS working framework.
- Support for internationalization is significant.
- Java is proposed to be appropriate for composing applications for both facilitated and installed frameworks.

Other structure objectives are talked about straightaway.

Strong Type Checking

Java is a solid kind language. Each factor that is characterized should be appended to an information type. A model is demonstrated as follows.

Model 2: The accompanying project shows a solid composing model for the Java programming language.

open class HelloWorld

```
{
open static void main(String[] args) {
int i=5;
```

```
System.out.println("The estimation of I is "+i);

}

}
```

You don't have to comprehend the total program for the time being, however we should simply have a brief glance at 2 lines of the code.

1) int i=5;

Here we are characterizing something known as a variable, which is utilized to hold a worth. The worth that can be put away relies upon the information type. In this model we are stating that 'I' is of the sort 'int' or Integer, which is a number of information esteem.

2) System.out.println("The estimation of I is "+i)

Here we print the estimation of 'I' by methods for the System.out.println explanation. On the off chance that we didn't proclaim 'I' as a number worth, we would then get the underneath mistake on the off chance that we needed to accumulate the program.

HelloWorld.java:5: blunder: can't discover image

```
System.out.println("The estimation of I is "+i);

^
```

Image: variable I

area: class HelloWorld

1 blunder

Array Bounds Checking

At runtime, Java will check whether the cluster has the necessary number of qualities characterized. In the event that one attempts to get to a worth which is beyond the exhibit, a special case will be tossed. A model is demonstrated as follows.

Model 3: The accompanying project is utilized to exhibit cluster limits checking.

open class HelloWorld

```
{

open static void main(String[] args) {

int[] array1 = new int[2];

array1[0] = 1;

array1[1] = 2;

array1[2] = 3;

}

}
```

You don't have to comprehend the total program for the time being, yet we should simply have a brief glance at the accompanying lines of the code.

```
1) int[] array1 = new int[2];
```

Here we are proclaiming an exhibit, which is a lot of whole number qualities. The estimation of '2' implies that we can just store two qualities in the exhibit.

```
2) array1[0] = 1;

array1[1] = 2;

array1[2] = 3;
```

With this code we can see that we are allocating 3 qualities to the cluster. At the point when you run this program, you will get a blunder on the grounds that the program will see that the exhibit has left its greatest passable limits of two. You will get the underneath mistake at runtime.

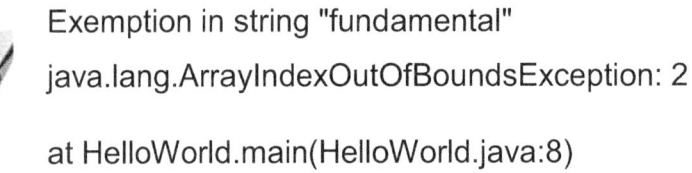

Exemption in string "fundamental"
java.lang.ArrayIndexOutOfBoundsException: 2

at HelloWorld.main(HelloWorld.java:8)

CHAPTER - 2

GET READY FOR JAVA

Let us begin by looking at the basic concepts and operations of the Java programming language. Java bears the unique distinction of operating as a modernized programming language but also as a platform. The programming language component of Java is centered on the aspect of writing instructions and compiling commands. The process begins with writing a source code in a plain text file that ends with the *.java* extension. This is followed by the deployment of the Javac compiler that converts the files into *.class* format. The *.class* file hosts bytecodes — that is, the specific language that the Java Virtual Machine (JVM) runs on.

The Java platform, on the other hand, is the general environment - be it software or hardware - that hosts program operations. The one outstanding uniqueness of the Java platform is that, unlike other platforms, it strictly operates as software that has capabilities for running on top of other platforms that are hardware-driven. The Java platform comprises the JVM and the Java API for anchoring platform applications and exposing the requisite software development tools, respectively.

Java is present in the software of most of the devices, gadgets, automated systems, and a large variety of information technology equipment that people interact with every other day. Java powers many apps in mobile devices, games, and software programs found in enterprise solutions as well as other types of web content. It could be easily described as the heartbeat of almost all types of network-based applications. Java operates as an object-oriented programming (OOP) platform. This means that Java is written on the basis of standard objects and class parameters.

The convenience of deploying Java lies on its compatibility with most OS platforms including Windows, Mac OS,

Linux, and Solaris OS, among others. Java's flexible programmatic features are crucial to the implementation of innovations in the Web and in computing environments. The portability and platform-independence attributes have been the driving force behind its relevance through the years and its growth into a leading programming language. The Java architecture consists of three major components including the Java Development Kit (JDK), the Java Runtime Environment (JRE), and the JVM.

Java Development Kit

The JDK provides the tools needed to build, test, and monitor robust Java-anchored applications. It allows developers to access software components and compile applications during Java programming operations. For example, a developer needs a JDK-powered environment to be able to write applets or implement methods.

Since the JDK more or less performs the operations of a Software Development Kit (SDK), one could easily confuse the scope and operations of the two items. Whereas the JDK is specific to the Java programming language, an SDK has broader applicability. But a JDK still operates as a component of an SDK in a program development environment. This means that a developer would still need an SDK to provide certain tools with broader operational characteristics and that are not available within the JDK domain. Developer documentation and debugging utilities as well as application servers are some of the crucial tools that an SDK supplies to a Java programming environment.

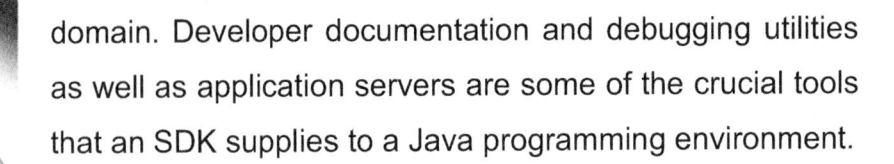

The scope of JDK deployment depends on the nature of the tasks at hand, the supported versions, and the Java edition that is in use. For example, the Java Platform, Standard Edition (Java SE) Development Kit is designed for use with the Java Standard Edition. The Java Platform, Enterprise Edition (Java EE) and the Java Platform, Macro Edition (Java ME) are the other major subsets of the JDK. Details of each of these Java editions are described in detail in the subtopics below. The JDK has been a free platform since 2007 when it was uploaded to the OpenJDK portal. Its open-source status facilitates collaborations and allows communities of software developers to clone, hack, or contribute ideas for advancements and upgrades.

Java SE

The Java SE powers a wide variety of desktop and server applications. It supports the testing and deployment of the Java programming language within the development environment of these applications. Some of the documentations associated with the recent releases of Java SE include an advanced management console feature and a revamped set of Java deployment rules.

Java SE 13.0.1 is the latest JDK version for the Java SE platform at the time of writing this book.

The Java SE SDK is equipped with the core JRE capabilities alongside a portfolio of tools, class libraries, and implementation technologies that are designed for use in the development of desktop applications. These tools range from simple objects and types for Java program implementations to advanced class parameters that are suited for building applications with networking capabilities and impenetrable security characteristics. Java programmers can also apply this particular JDK on the development of Java applications used to simplify access to databases or to enhance GUI properties.

Java EE

The Java EE platform is an open-source product that is developed through the collaborative efforts of members of the Java community worldwide. Java EE is closely related to the Java SE because the former is built on top of the latter. This particular software is integrated with transformative innovations that are designed for use in enterprise solutions. The features and advancements that are introduced in new releases often reflect the inputs, requirements, and requests of members of the Java community. The Java EE actually offers more than twenty implementations that are complaint with Java programming.

The Java EE SDK is meant for use in the construction of applications for large-scale operations. Just as its name suggests, this particular Java SDK was created to provide support for enterprise software solutions. The JDK features a powerful API and runtime properties that Java programmers require to build applications with scalable and networkable functionalities. Developers in need of developing multi-tiered applications could find this JDK useful as well.

Java EE's revised design provides enhanced technologies for enterprise solutions as well as modernized applications for security and management purposes. The release features several advancements that included greater REST API capabilities provided through the Client, JSON Binding, Servlet, and Security APIs. This version also features the Date and Time API as well as the Streams API, according to information published in the Oracle Corporate website as of December 2019.

Java ME

The Java ME platform deploys simplicity, portability, and dynamism to provide a versatile environment for building applications for small gadgets and devices. Java ME is known for having an outstanding application development environment, thanks to its interactive and user-friendly navigation interfaces as well as built-in capabilities for implementing networking concepts. It is largely associated with the Internet of Things (IoT) and is useful when building applications designed for built-in technologies or connected devices that could be used to invent or implement futuristic concepts. Java ME's portability and runtime attributes make it suitable for use in software applications for wearable gadgets, cell phones, cameras, sensors, and printers, among other items and equipment.

The Java ME SDK is equipped with the requisite tools meant for use within an independent environment when developing software applications, testing functionalities, and implementing device simulations. According to information published in the Oracle Corporate website as of 2019, this JDK is well suited for accommodating "the Connected Limited Device Configuration (CLDC)" technology alongside "the Connected Device Configuration (CDC)" functionality. This results in a single and versatile environment for developing applications.

There are several other Java ME solutions that support the deployment of the Java programming language in applications. Java ME Embedded provides a runtime environment integrating IoT capabilities in devices, while the Java ME embedded client facilitates the construction of software solutions that run and optimize the functionality of built-in programs. Java for Mobile makes use of the CLDC and the stack of Java ME developer tools to create innovative features for mobile devices.

Java Runtime Environment

Remember that there are certain conditions that must prevail for Java applications to run efficiently. The JRE contains the ingredients responsible for creating these requisite conditions. This includes the JVM and its corresponding files and class attributes. Although JRE operates as a component of the JDK, it is capable of operating independently, especially if the tasks are limited to run rather than build application instructions.

The JRE lends important operational properties to different programs in the Java programming ecosystem. For example, a program is considered self-contained if it runs an independent JRE within it. This means that a program does not depend on other programs to access the JRE. This independence makes it possible for a program to achieve compatibility with different OS platforms.

Java Virtual Machine

The JVM operates as a specification for implementing Java in computer programs. It is the driving force behind the platform-independence characteristics of the Java language. This status is accentuated by JVM's status as a program that is executed by other programs. The programs written to interact with and execute the JVM see it as a machine. It is for this reason that similar sets, libraries, and interfaces are used to write Java programs to be able to match every single JVM implementation to a particular OS. This facilitates the translation or interpretation of Java programs into runtime instructions in the local OS, and thereby eliminating the need for platform dependence in Java programming.

As a developer you must be wary of the vulnerability your development environment and applications have to cyber-attacks and other threats. The JVM provides enhanced security features that protect you from such threats. The solid security foundation is attributable to its built-in syntax and structure limitations that reside in the operational codes of class files. But this does not translate to limitations on the scope of class files that the JVM can accommodate. The JVM actually accepts a variety of class files so long as they can be validated to be safe and secure. Therefore, the JVM is a viable complementary alternative for developing software in other programming languages.

The JVM is often included as a ported feature in a wide variety of software applications and hardware installations. It is implemented through algorithms that are determined by Oracle or any other provider. As such, the JVM provides an open implementation platform. The JVM actually contains the runtime instance as the core property that anchors its command operations. For example, the creation of a JVM instance simply involves writing an instruction in the command prompt that, in turn, runs the class properties of Java.

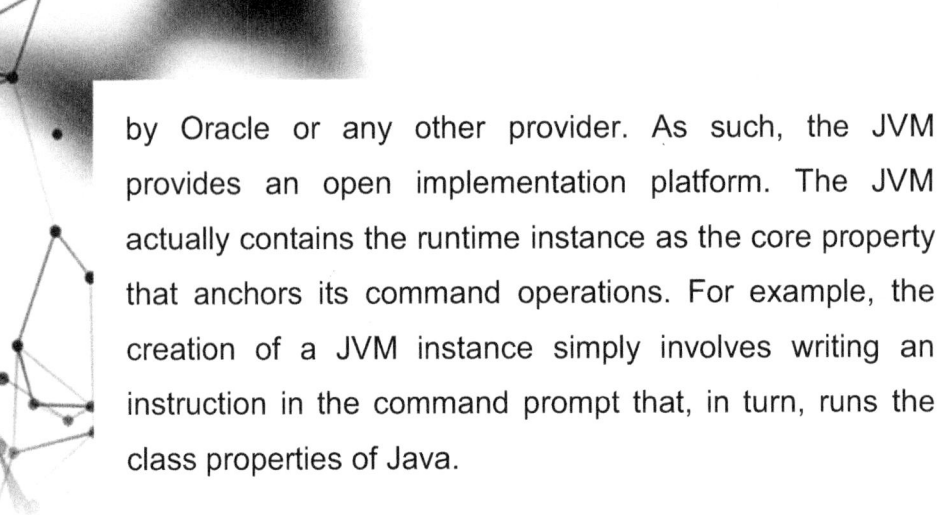

A Java programmer needs to be familiar with the key areas of JVM such as the classloader and the data unit for runtime operations as well as the engine that is responsible for executing programs. There are also performance-related components, such as the garbage collector and the heap dimension tool, that are equally important to the deployment of the JVM. There is a close affiliation between the JVM and bytecodes.

CHAPTER - 3

GETTING READY FOR JAVA

Bytecodes

Bytecodes are essentially JVM commands that are contained in a class file alongside other information that include the symbol table. They operate as background language programs responsible for facilitating the interpretation and execution of JVM operations. Bytecodes are actually the substitutes to native codes because Java does not provide the latter. The structure of the JVM register is such that it contains methods which, in turn, accommodate bytecode streams that is, sets of instructions for the JVM. In other words, each Java class has methods within it and the class file loading process executes a single bytecode stream for any given method. The activation of a method automatically triggers a bytecode the moment a program begins to run.

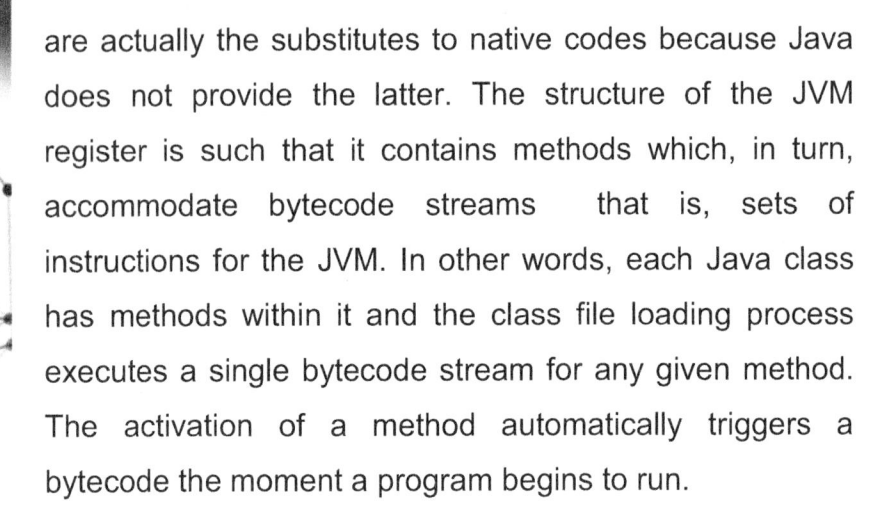

The other important feature of bytcodes is the Just-in-time (JIT) compiler that operates during the runtime operations for compiling codes that can be executed. The feature actually exists as a HotSpot JIT compiler within the JVM ecosystem. It executes codes concurrently with the Java runtime operations because it has the ability to perform at optimized levels and the flexibility to scale and accommodate growing traffic of instructions. The JIT compiler required frequent tuning to rid it of redundant programs and refresh its memory. Tuning was a necessary procedure that ensured the JIT compiler delivered optimum performance. However, the frequent upgrades in the newer versions of Java gradually introduced automated memory refreshing mechanisms that eliminated the need for regular tuning.

Bytecodes can be either primitive types, flexible types, or stack-based. According to Venners (1996), there are seven parameters of primitive data including *byte*, *char*, *double*, *float*, *int*, *long*, and *short*. The *boolean* parameter is also a widely used primitive type, taking the tally to eight. Each of the eight parameters is meant to help developers deploy variables that can be acted upon by the bytecodes. Bytecode streams actually express these parameters of the primitive types in the form of operands. This ends up designating the larger and more powerful parameters to the higher levels of the bytes' hierarchy, with the smaller ones occupying the lower levels of the hierarchy in a descending order.

Java opcodes are similarly crucial components of the primitive types, thanks to their role of classifying operands. This role ensures that operands retain their state, thereby eliminating the need for an operand identification interface in the JVM. The JVM is able to speed up processes because it is capable of multitasking while accommodating multiple opcodes that deliver domicile variables into stacks. Opcodes are also useful for processing and defining the value parameters for stack-based bytecodes. According to Venners (1996), this could be an implicit constant value, an operand value, or a value derived from a constant pool.

The Upsides of Java

- Java epitomizes simplicity in programming, thanks to its user-friendly interface for learning, writing, deployment, and implementation.
- Java's core architecture is designed to facilitate ease of integration and convenience of use within the development environment.
- Java is platform-independent and readily portable, making it suitable for multitasking and use across software applications.
- The object-oriented characteristics of Java support the creation of programs with standard features and codes that can be redeployed.
- Java's networking capabilities make it easier for programmers to create software solutions for shared computing environments.
- The close relationship between Java, the C++, and the C languages makes it easier for anyone with knowledge of the other two languages to learn Java.
- Java's automated garbage collection provides continuous memory protection, making it convenient for programmers to eliminate security vulnerabilities while writing codes.
- Java's architecture is flexible for the implementation of multithreading programs.

- Java is readily reusable, thanks to the ability to redeploy classes using the interface or inheritance features.

The Downsides of Java

- Since Java is not a native application, it runs at lower speeds compared to other programming languages.
- Java may also lack consistency in the processing and displaying of graphics. For example, the ordinary appearance of the graphical user interface (GUI) in Java-based applications is quite different and of lower standards compared to the GUI output of native software applications.
- Java's garbage collection, a feature that manages memory efficiency, may interfere with speed and performance whenever it runs as a background application.

JDK Download and Configuration

Most of the widely referenced resources for beginners in Java programming often dive straight into the compiling and running procedures of a Java program. However, one of the major challenges that beginners face is getting lost the moment they are unable to configure Java in the command prompt. In most cases, the command prompt displays error messages indicating the unavailability of the Java program that a newbie is trying to launch. That happens when the path for the Java program has not been set in the command prompt. To avoid such setbacks, perform the initial launch procedures as follows. This guide takes a different approach by beginning from the configuration and launch phase of Java in the command prompt.

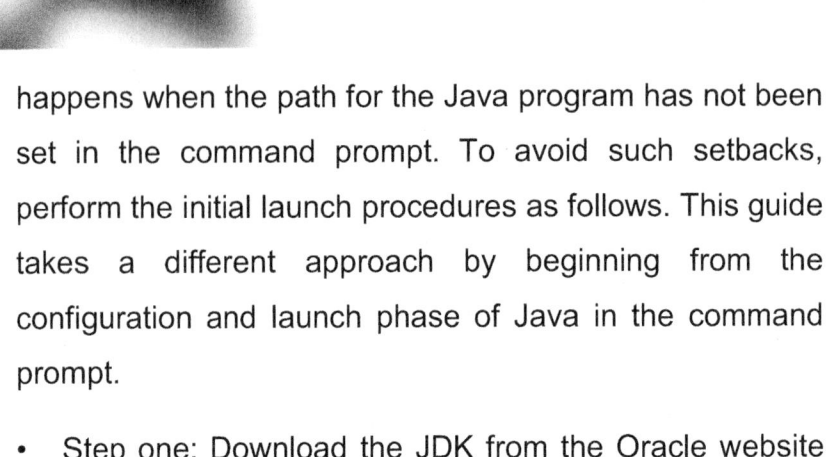

- Step one: Download the JDK from the Oracle website and save it in the C drive of your computer. The Oracle download page provides the download links for the latest release and the earlier releases as well as other developer resources for Java programming. This guide is using the jdk-13.0.1 release in Windows 7.
- Step two: Press the Windows and the R keys to launch the pop up window for running programs.
- Step three: Type the phrase cmd.exe in the field and press OK to launch the command prompt.

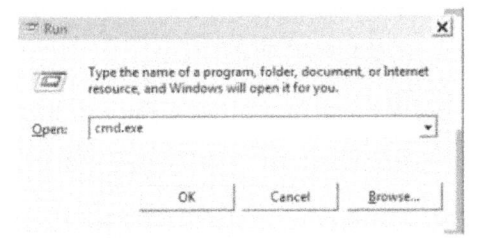

![Run dialog box with cmd.exe typed in the Open field]

- Step four: Crosscheck the command prompt window that pops up to ensure that it contains the relevant descriptions. The users name will depend on the one set on your computer.

- Step five: Enter these particulars — Set path= — right after the > sign (do not enter space in between). Locate the folder where you saved the JDK download and copy the path of the JDK. The file path for this guide was C:\Program Files\Java\jdk-13.0.1\bin. Paste the path right after the = sign and press Enter. This procedure sets the path for your JDK as follows:

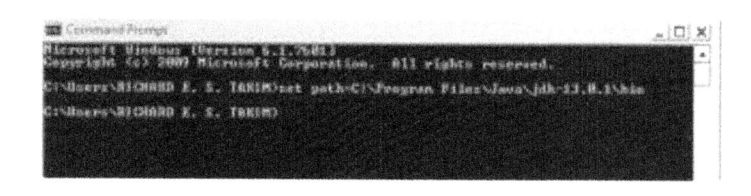

You can be sure at this point that your JDK is properly downloaded and configured in the system. You can now proceed to the next phase of writing your first Java program. However, the above procedure is a temporary solution because you will have to set the path every time you launch the command prompt. It is worth understanding it as a beginner because it could be helpful in the initialization of your Java programs.

Compile and Run the First Java Program

The compilation of the first Java programs for beginners often revolves around the "Hello World" and "My First Java

Program" phrases. That does not mean that those are the only phrases that you can use to compile your programs. You can use any names as long as you get the coding right and save your files in the recommended format. The preferred phrase for this guide is "My Simple Java Program". You need a text editor, preferably Notepad, to be able to compile your first Java program.

- Step one: Create and name a folder in your preferred location. This folder will provide storage for both your Notepad document and the class file that will be created. For purposes of simplicity, this guide has named the folder MySimpleJavaProgram.

- Step two: Open Notepad and type the following instructions.

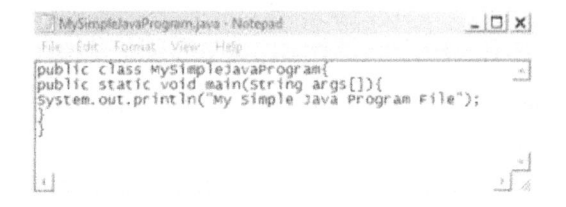

```
MySimpleJavaProgram.java - Notepad
File Edit Format View Help
public class MySimpleJavaProgram{
public static void main(string args[]){
System.out.println("My Simple Java Program File");
}
```

- Step three: Save the file in the destination folder. Remember the file name must be saved in a .java format. For example, the file name for this guide would be MyFirstJavaProgram.java. Change the file type from Text Document to All Files.

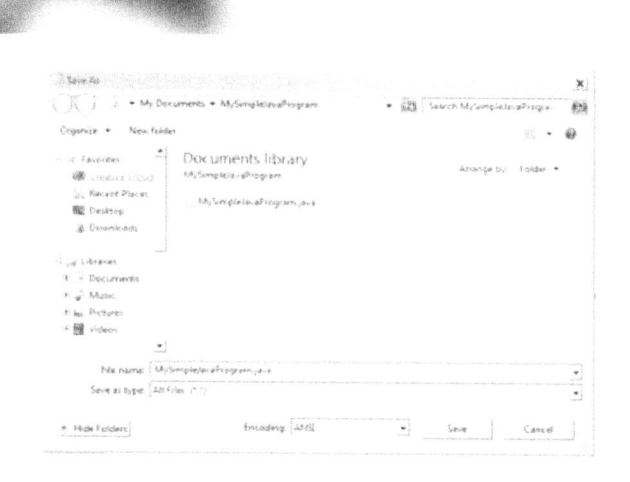

- Step four: Open a command prompt and change the file path to match the path of the compiled Java program in the destination folder. Looking at the example in this guide, the MySimpleJavaProgram.java folder is stored in Documents in the MySimpleJavaProgram folder. Therefore, the initial step here would be to change the directory to Documents by typing >cd documents and pressing Enter.

Microsoft Windows [Version 6.1.7601]

Copyright (c) 2009 Microsoft Corporation. All rights reserved.

C:\Users\RICHARD E. S. TAKIM>cd documents

- Step five: Type >cd MySimpleJavaProgram to change the directory to the destination folder and press Enter.

Microsoft Windows [Version 6.1.7601]

Copyright (c) 2009 Microsoft Corporation. All rights reserved.

C:\Users\RICHARD E. S. TAKIM>cd documents

C:\Users\RICHARD E. S. TAKIM\Documents>cd MySimpleJavaProgram

- Step six: Proceed to type >javac MySimpleJavaProgram.java and press Enter to compile the program.

Microsoft Windows [Version 6.1.7601]

Copyright (c) 2009 Microsoft Corporation. All rights reserved.

C:\Users\RICHARD E. S. TAKIM>cd documents

C:\Users\RICHARD E. S. TAKIM\Documents>cd MySimpleJavaProgram

C:\Users\RICHARD E. S. TAKIM\Documents\MySimpleJavaProgram>javac MySimpleJavaProgram.java

- Step seven: If successful, the procedures above will result in a command prompt window that resembles the one below. The procedure will effectively have created a class file of the program.

Important Program Compilation Tips

In step two, although many resources have the second and third lines indented, such indentation does not affect the processing of the coding when using the command prompt. In some cases, the indentation usually occurs as a default feature in some integrated development environments (IDEs).

In step three, there are occasions when the .txt extension could remain hidden and attached on a saved file name as .java.txt. Such a mishap would mean that the command prompt would not be able to trace the file response when you finally run the javac program. To avoid the .txt format, click Computer > Organize > Folder and Search Options > View. Uncheck the "Hide extensions for known file types" as demonstrated below.

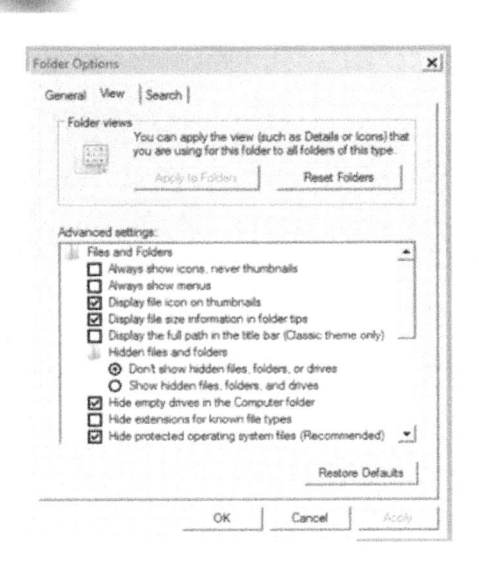

In step four, you could experience trouble locating your file or having the command prompt generating warnings that a file cannot be found or recognized. To solve such problems, you would need to confirm whether or not the file has been loaded into the command prompt directory. Open the command prompt and change directory to the location of your program's destination folder, press Enter and type DIR. For example type >cd Documents, press Enter and then type >DIR. Scan through the results to find out if the destination folder or the program file is loaded. For example, the results below show that the MySimpleJavaProgram is available in the directory.

CHAPTER - 4

VARIABLES AND OPERATORS

Since you know about NetBeans and have some essential comprehension of a Java program, how about we get down to the genuine stuff. In this part, you'll gain proficiency with about factors and administrators. In particular, you'll realize what factors are and how to name, pronounce and introduce them. You'll likewise find out about the normal tasks that we can perform on them.

What are Variables?

Variables are names given to information that we have to store and control in our projects. For example, assume your program needs to store the age of a client. To do that, we can name this information client Age and proclaim the variable client Age utilizing the accompanying articulation:

int client Age;

This assertion articulation first expresses the information kind of the variable, trailed by its name. The information sort of a variable alludes to the kind of information that the variable will store, (for example, regardless of whether it's a number or a bit of text). In our model, the information type is int, which alludes to whole numbers.

The name of our variable is client Age.

After you proclaim the variable userAge, your program will apportion a specific zone of your PC's memory space to store this information. You would then be able to get to and alter this information by alluding to it by its name, userAge.

First Data types in java

There are eight fundamental information types that are predefined in Java. These are known as crude information types.

The initial 4 information types are for putting away whole numbers (for example numbers with no fragmentary parts). They are as per the following:

Byte

The byte information type is utilized for putting away numbers from - 128 to 127. It utilizes 1 byte of extra room (this is known as the width or the size of the information type). We ordinarily utilize the byte information type if extra room is a worry or on the off chance that we are sure the estimation of the variable won't surpass the - 128 to 127 territory.

For example, we can utilize the byte information type to store the age of a client as it is impossible that the client's age will ever surpass 127 years of age.

Short

The short information type utilizes 2 bytes of extra room and has a scope of - 32768 to 32767.

Int

The int information type utilizes 4 bytes of extra room and has a scope of -231 (-2147483648) to 231-1 (2147483647). It is the most regularly utilized information type for putting away numbers as it has the most commonsense range.

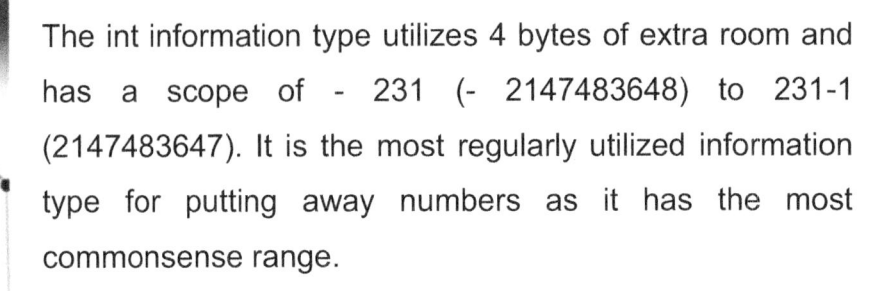

Long

The long information type utilizes 8 bytes of extra room and has a scope of -263 to 263-1. It is once in a while utilized except if you truly need to store an exceptionally huge whole number, (for example, the quantity of occupants on Earth). So as to indicate a long worth, you need to include the addition "L" to the furthest limit of the number. We'll speak progressively about postfixes in the following segment.

Notwithstanding having information types for putting away whole numbers, we likewise have information types for putting away gliding point numbers (for example numbers with partial parts). They are:

Buoy

The buoy information type utilizes 4 bytes of capacity and has a scope of around negative 3.40282347 x 1038 to positive 3.40282347 x 1038. It has an accuracy of around 7 digits. This implies on the off chance that you use buoy to store a number like 1.23456789 (10 digits), the number will be adjusted to roughly 7 digits (for example 1.234568).

Twofold

The twofold information type utilizes 8 bytes of capacity and has a scope of around negative 1.79769313486231570 x 10308 to positive 1.79769313486231570 x 10308, with an accuracy of roughly 15 digits.

As a matter of course, at whatever point you determine a gliding point number in Java, it is naturally viewed as a twofold, not a buoy. In the event that you need Java to treat the skimming point number as a buoy, you need to include an addition "F" to the furthest limit of the number.

Except if memory space is a worry, you ought to consistently utilize a twofold rather than a buoy as it is increasingly exact.

Other than the six information types referenced above, Java has two progressively crude information types. They are:

Scorch

Scorch represents the character and is utilized to store single Unicode characters, for example, 'A', '%', '@' and 'p' and so on. It utilizes 2 bytes of memory.

Boolean

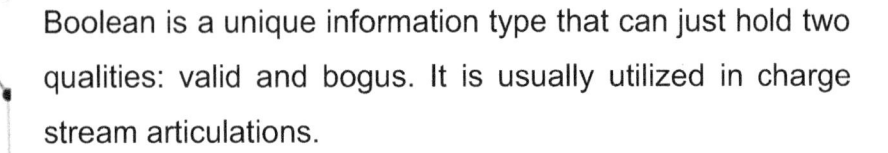

Boolean is a unique information type that can just hold two qualities: valid and bogus. It is usually utilized in charge stream articulations.

Naming a Variable

A variable name in Java can just contain letters, numbers, underscores (_) or the dollar sign ($). In any case, the primary character can't be a number. Subsequently, you can name your factors _userName, $username, username or userName2 however not 2userName.

The show, be that as it may, is to consistently start your variable names with a letter, not "$" or "_". Also, the dollar sign character is never utilized when naming a variable (in spite of the fact that it isn't in fact wrong to utilize it).

Variable names ought to be short however important, intended to show to the easygoing peruser the aim of its utilization. It bodes well to name your factors client Name, client Age and client Number, rather than n, an and un.

What's more, there are some held words that you can't use as a variable name since they as of now have pre-doled out implications in Java. These saved words incorporate words like System, if, while and so on.

It is normal practice to utilize camel packaging when naming factors in Java. Camel packaging is the act of composing compound words with blended packaging, underwriting the main letter of each word aside from the primary word (for example thisIsAVariableName).

At last, factor names are case touchy. thisIsAVariableName isn't equivalent to thisisavariablename.

Initializing a Variable

Each time you proclaim another variable, you have to give it an underlying worth. This is known as instating the variable. You can change the estimation of the variable in your program later.

There are two different ways to introduce a variable. You can introduce it at the purpose of affirmation or instate it in a different explanation.

The code beneath shows how you can instate factors at the purpose of announcement (line numbers on the left are included for reference and are not part of the code).

```
1 Byte userAge = 20;

2 Short numberOfStudents = 45;

3 Int numberOfEmployees = 500;
```

```
4 Long numberOfInhabitants = 21021313012678L;

5 Float hourlyRate = 60.5F;

6 twofold numberOfHours = 5120.5;

7 Char grade = 'A';

8 Boolean advance = valid;

9 Byte level = 2, userExperience = 5;
```

As referenced above, so as to indicate a long worth, you need to include the addition "L" to the furthest limit of the number. Consequently, on line 4 when we introduced numberOfInhabitants, we included "L" to the furthest limit of the number. In the event that we don't do that, the compiler will gripe that the number is excessively huge and give us a blunder.

Also, when we introduced the variable hourlyRate on line 6, we included the postfix "F". This is on the grounds that as a matter of course, any drifting point number is treated as a twofold by Java. We have to include the postfix "F" to demonstrate to the compiler that hourlyRate is of buoy information type.

At long last, while introducing a burn information type, we have to encase the character in single statements as appeared on line 9.

On line 12, we see a case of how you can announce and introduce two factors of similar information type in one explanation. The two factors are isolated by a comma, and there is no compelling reason to express the information sort of the subsequent variable.

The models above show how you can introduce a variable at the purpose of the presentation. On the other hand, you can decide to announce and introduce a variable in two separate proclamations as demonstrated as follows:

```
byte year;/proclaim the variable first

year = 20;/introduce it later
```

Exercise

As a snappy exercise, we should take a portion of the data that we have found out about factors and make an adding machine that will deal with including numbers for us. The main thing we will do is to proclaim three factors; one to store your incentive in, one that will speak to which number we include first, and afterward one to speak to the second number you need to include. We will proclaim these factors as twofold so it is simpler to include in decimal focuses later. Our code is going to look something like this:

```
double a = 0;/stores estimation of expansion
```

```
double b = 3.55;/first number to include

double c = 52.6;/second number to include
```

Presently that these are totally pronounced, you will have the option to type in their variable to find the correct solution. So how about we set the estimation of a with the goal that it is equivalent to when b and c are included, and afterward have the framework print out what the estimation of a winds up being. Type in the accompanying to get this to deal with your condition:

```
a = b + c;

System.out.println(a);
```

At the point when this program is running, you will find the solution 56.15. With this basic code, you have chipped away at making your first adding machine. Evaluate a couple of various numbers and become accustomed to working around with this alternative by changing a portion of the information types, including some more numbers, and figuring out how it feels to work out a portion of these codes with factors in them.

Assignment Operator, Basic Operator

The = sign in programming has an alternate importance from the = sign we learned in Math. In programming, the = sign is known as a task administrator. It implies we are allotting the incentive on the correct side of the = sign to the variable on the left.

In programming, the announcements x = y and y = x have altogether different implications.

Befuddled? A model will probably clear this up.

Assume we proclaim two factors x and y as follows:

```
int x = 5;

int y = 10;

In the event that you compose

x = y;
```

Your Math instructor is likely going to be agitated with you since x isn't equivalent to y. In any case, in programming, this is fine.

This announcement implies we are appointing the estimation of y to x. It is okay to allot the estimation of a variable to another variable. In our model, the estimation of x is currently changed to 10 while the estimation of y stays unaltered. As it were, x = 10 and y = 10 at this point.

In the event that we currently change the estimations of x and y to 3 and 20 separately by composing

```
x = 3;
```

```
y = 20;

What's more, compose

y = x;
```

We are allotting the estimation of x to the variable y. Henceforth, y gets 3 while the estimation of x stays unaltered (for example y = 3, x = 3 at this point).

Other Operators

Other than doling out an underlying incentive to a variable or relegating another variable to it, we can likewise play out the typical scientific procedure on factors. Fundamental administrators in Java incorporate +, - , *,/and % which speak to expansion, deduction, increase, division and modulus individually.

Model

```
Assume x = 7, y = 2

Expansion: x + y = 9

Deduction: x - y = 5

Duplication: x*y = 14
```

Division: x/y = 3 (adjusts down the response to the closest number)

Modulus: x%y = 1 (gives the rest of 7 is separated by 2)

In Java, division offers a number response if both x and y are whole numbers. Be that as it may, if either x or y is a non-number, we will get a non-whole number answer.

For example,

7/2 = 3

7.0/2 = 3.5

7/2.0 = 3.5

7.0/2.0 = 3.5

In the principal case, when a whole number is isolated by another number, you find a number as the solution. The decimal part of the appropriate response, assuming any, is shortened. Henceforth, we get 3 rather than 3.5.

In every single other case, the outcome is a non-number as at any rate one of the operands is a non-whole number.

Note that 7.0 isn't equivalent to 7 in Java. The former is a gliding point number while the last is a whole number.

Greater Assignment Operators

Other than the = administrator, there are a couple of greater task administrators in Java (and most programming dialects). These incorporate administrators like +=, - = and *=.

Assume we have the variable x, with an underlying estimation of 10. On the off chance that we need to increase x by 2, we can compose

```
x = x + 2;
```

The program will initially assess the articulation on the right (x + 2) and relegate the response to one side. So in the long run x gets 12.

Rather than composing x = x + 2, we can likewise compose x += 2 to communicate a similar importance. The += administrator is a shorthand that joins the task administrator with the expansion administrator. Subsequently, x += 2 essentially implies x = x + 2.

So also, on the off chance that we need to do a deduction, we can compose x = x - 2 or x - = 2. Similar works for all the 5 administrators referenced in the area above.

Most programming dialects likewise have the ++ and − administrators. The ++ administrator is utilized when you need to expand the estimation of a variable by 1. For example, assume

```
int x = 2;

In the event that you compose

x++;
```

The estimation of x gets 3.

There is no compelling reason to utilize the = administrator when you utilize the ++ administrator. The announcement x++; is comparable to

x = x + 1;

The ++ administrator can be put before or behind the variable name. This influences the request wherein assignments are performed.

Assume we have a whole number named counter. On the off chance that we compose

System.out.println(counter++);

The program first prints the first estimation of counter before augmenting counter by 1. At the end of the day, it executes the errands in a specific order

System.out.println(counter);

counter = counter + 1;

Then again, in the event that we compose

System.out.println(++counter);

The program's first additions counter by 1 preceding printing the new estimation of counter. At the end of the day, it executes the errands in a specific order

```
counter = counter + 1;

System.out.println(counter);
```

Notwithstanding the ++ administrator, we likewise have the − administrator (two short signs). This administrator diminishes the estimation of the variable by 1.

Type Casting In Java

Now and again in our program, it is important to change over starting with one information type then onto the next, for example, from a twofold to an int. This is known as type throwing.

In the event that we need to change over a littler information type into a bigger information type, we don't have to do anything expressly. For example, the code beneath allots a short (2 bytes) to a twofold (8 bytes). This is known as an extending crude change and doesn't require any exceptional code on our part.

```
short age = 10;

twofold myDouble = age;
```

In any case, in the event that we need to allocate a bigger information type to a littler information type, we have to demonstrate it unequivocally utilizing a couple of enclosure. This is known as a narrowing crude transformation. The model underneath shows how it tends to be finished.

```
int x = (int) 20.9;
```

Here, we can throwing a twofold (8 bytes) into an int (4 bytes).

Narrowing change isn't sheltered and ought to be kept away from except if completely important. This is on the grounds that narrowing transformation can bring about lost information. At the point when we cast 20.9 into an int, the subsequent worth is 20, not 21. The decimal segment is shortened after the transformation.

We can likewise cast a twofold into a buoy. Review that we referenced before that all non-whole numbers are treated as twofold as a matter of course in Java? On the off chance that we need to allocate a number like 20.9 to a buoy, we have to include an addition 'F' to the number. Another approach to do it is to utilize a cast, this way: Coast num1 = (drift) 20.9;

The estimation of num1 will be 20.9.

Notwithstanding throwing between numeric sorts, we can likewise do different kinds of throwing.

CHAPTER - 5

ARRAYS AND STRING

What are Strings

A string is a sequence of characters and can also be known as a string. To declare a string in JAVA, simply use the keyword "string"

Then name your chain as you like

Then put an equal symbol after

Then, enclose double strings in double quotes, and print it anyway:

String sample = "Welcome Ron";

System.out.println (sample)

String Methods

In the above example, there are two variables **message** and **s** of **String** type. The statement *message = s + "Ron";* will append the string **"World"** to the contents of **s** and save it in **message**. Hence, message will now hold **"Welcome Ron"**.

Arrays

A table is similar to a variable, but can store more than one value at a time; the only condition is that although you can store more than one value in a table it must be the same value type

For example, you could store 10 integers in a table, but if you want to store 5 integers and 5 doubles, you won't be able to.

This is one way to declare a table: int [] RonArray = {4, 62,1,54,3};

Another way is: int myinarray2 [] = {4,62,1,54,3 τρόπος This is a good way, but it is not the preferred way to declare a table

There are three more ways to declare matrices

1.int[] RonArray = new int[3];

2.int[] RonArray = {1,2,3};

3.int[] RonArray = new int []{1,2,3};

Array Methods

The int [] RonArray section indicates that the table is from the original int variable denoted by the RonArray name or reference. The square brackets [] indicate that they are a reference to a table. The new section int [7] indicates that a new table object is being created. The number in parentheses means that the length of the table equals 7. The RonArray element index consists of the numbers 0, 1, 2, 3, 4, 5, and 6. There are a total of seven elements. To find the element, for example, at index 2, we use the name of the table and in parentheses the index of the element: RonArray [2]. In our example, all seven elements are equal to 0 because they have not been initialized. If a variable of type int is not initialized, its value is by default equal to 0.

The program in Example 1 writes seven zeros to the standard output: 0000000

int [] RonArray = new int [7]

The following code changes the value of the fourth element in the table to 11. Remember that the first element of the index is 0.

```
intArray [3] = 11
```

Try importing the java.util.Arrays package from the Java Standard API to learn how to sort the elements of a table.

Primitive Types

Primitive data types are data types that Java has already defined for you. This means that you can't use them as names for variables, classes, etc. There are only eight primitive data types defined in Java:

- boolean – boolean data types can only store true or false values and therefore has a very small size of 1 bit.
- byte – byte data types can store integers with a size of only 8 bits.
- short – short data types can also store integers with a larger size of 16 bits
- char – char can store Unicode characters, which would mean one letter/number/symbol, with a size of 16 bits.
- int – int is the most commonly used data type because it can store integers with the standard size of 32 bits – enough to represent most of the integers you'd be using in standard programs.

- long – long is used when a program needs to store a really huge number that int can no longer store. With a size of 64 bits, it has twice the space that int has.
- float – float is used when you need to store numbers with decimal points. Like int it also has 32 bits of allocated space.
- double – double is used when float can no longer accommodate the size of a number with a decimal point. Like long it also has 64 bits of allocated space.

What's special about Java is that there's a special support for strings coming from the java.lang.String class. This means that you can easily create strings by typing a line of code like:

```
String sentence = "Welcome Ron !";
```

Remember though that String is not considered a primitive data type, but since its usage is somewhat similar anyway you might as well use it as such.

Reference Types

To utilize an array as a part of a system, you must declare a variable to reference the array. Besides this, you must determine the sort of array the variable can reference. Here is the syntax for declaring a variable of the type array:

```
datatype[] RonArray;
```

Sample Implementation:

The accompanying code bits are illustrations of this concept:

```
double[] RonArray;
```

Making Arrays

You can make an exhibit by utilizing the new operator with the accompanying statement:

```
RonArray = new datatype[sizeofarray];
```

The above declaration does two things:

- It makes an exhibit with the help of the new operator in the following manner:

```
new datatype[arraysize];
```

- It relegates the reference of the recently made array to the variable RonArray.

Proclaiming a array variable, making an exhibit, and doling out the reference of the show to the variable can be consolidated in one declaration, as appeared:

```
datatype[] RonArray = new datatype[sizeofarray];
```

On the other hand, you can also make clusters in the following manner:

```
datatype[] RonArray = {val0, val1, ..., valk};
```

The components of the array are gotten through the record. Array lists are 0-based; that is, they begin from 0 to go up to RonArray.length-1.

Sample Implementation:

The declaration shown below declares an array, RonArray, makes a cluster of 10 components of double type and doles out its reference to RonArray:

```
double[] RonArray = new double[10];
```

Handling Arrays

Project/Exercise

A string variable can be set once, at that point utilized commonly in a program. String factors make it simple to change a word or expression utilized ordinarily in a program.

Attempt It

Begin composing the following system:

1. Create another Java venture called Name Game and add DIYJava.jar to the undertaking.

2. Create another bundle called _____._____.namegame in the venture.
3. Create another class called NameGame, with superclass DIYWindow and with a stub for primary() and its constructors.
4. Add code to principle() to call the NameGame constructor.

Posting 3-1, from NameGame.java

bundle annette.godtland.namegame;

import com.godtsoft.diyjava.DIYWindow;

```
open class NameGame expands DIYWindow {

open NameGame() {

}

open static void main(String[] args) {

new _____;

}

}
```

Finished posting

1.   Print the "Jack be Nimble" nursery rhyme:

Jack be agile,

Jack be fast,

Jack bounce over the candle.

Posting 3-2, from NameGame.java

...

```
open NameGame() {

print("_____");

print("_____");

print("_____");

}
```

...

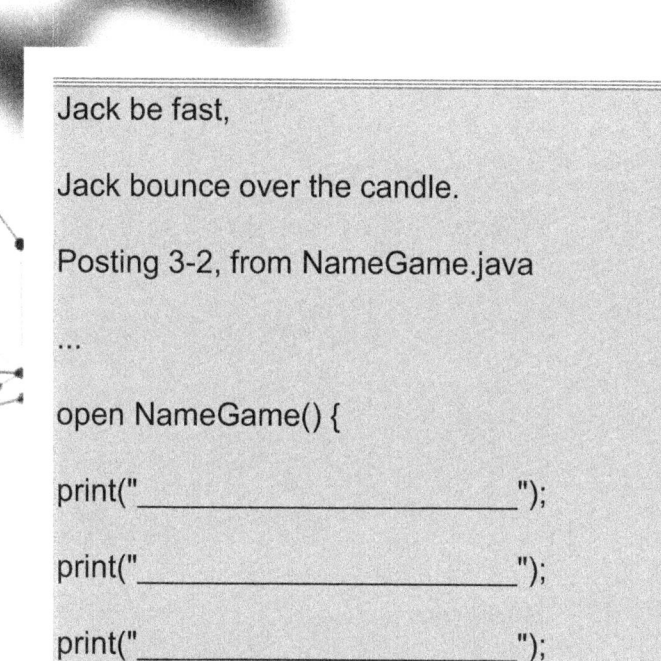

Finished posting

1. Add code to place Jack's name into a string called name.
2. Change the code to print name got together with " be deft."

Posting 3-3, from NameGame.java

...

```
open NameGame() {

String name = "Jack";
```

```
print(

name + "

be nimble,");

print("Jack be quick,");

print("Jack hop over the candlestick.");

}
```

...

Finished posting

1. Change the code to utilize your name with " be deft,".

Posting 3-4, from NameGame.java

...

```
open NameGame() {

String name = "

";

print(name + " be nimble,");

print("Jack be quick,");

print("Jack hop over the candlestick.");

}
```

...

Finished posting

1. How would you change the remainder of the lines so they likewise utilize your name rather than Jack's?

Posting 3-5, from NameGame.java

...

```
open NameGame() {

String name = "Annette";

print(name + " be nimble,");

print(
_____
);

print(
_____
);

}
```

...

Finished posting

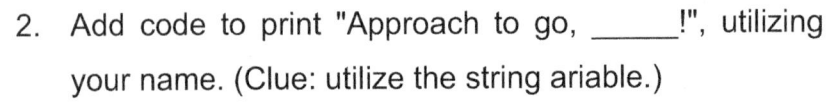

1. Add code after the nursery rhyme to print a clear line after the nursery rhyme.
2. Add code to print "Approach to go, _____!", utilizing your name. (Clue: utilize the string ariable.)

Posting 3-6, from NameGame.java

...

```
open NameGame() {

String name = "Annette";

print(name + " be nimble,");

print(name + " be quick,");

print(name + " bounce over the candlestick.");

print(

_____

);

print(

_____

);

}
```

...

CHAPTER - 6

PROGRAMMING CONTROL STATEMENT

While working in Java, you may come across times when you would need the program to make decisions. These decisions would be based on a combination of the conditions that you set and the input that the user gives to you. Depending on the conditional statement that you choose, the program will determine if the input is considered true or false based on the conditions that you set.

In technical language, these are called the conditional statements, but we can also call them the if, the if...else, or the switch statements. Each of these will work slightly differently. For example, the if statement will only have one option and is looking for the true input. If your user places in a true answer, the program will execute, usually with a statement that you placed in. With the if...else statement, you can place two conditions inside. If the input from the user is true, your user will see one answer, but if their input is false, your user can see a different answer.

Both of these are needed to help you to create some power inside of your code and gives you some control over the response of your program based on the input that the user places in. Let's take some time to look over these conditional statements and see what all they can do.

The If Statements

When working with the if statement, we are talking about a true and false method. This statement is going to decide whether the input of the user is considered true or false and then it will give the response that is needed based on the conditions you set. You will be able to choose the conditions that are true based on your program.

You can determine the statements that you would like to come out when the user puts in an answer that is considered true. But with the if statement, when the user puts in an answer that is false, the computer isn't going to show up anything. This is part of the limitations with the if statement; nothing is going to come up when the answer is false, such as when the user puts in the wrong answer to 2 + 2. A blank screen doesn't look that good when your user is on the program.

You may choose to just have a message come up if the person is older than 18. You would need to use the >=18 sign in the code and then add in the message that you would like. For example, if the person placed their age as 35, you could have the program provide the statement "Congratulations! You are able to participate!" and then it would go on to the next part of your code. On the other hand, if your user places their age as 16, the program would either end or it would move on to the next thing that you want to show up in your program.

The If...Else Statement

When you are working with the if statements, you are going to have some limitations to what the code is able to do. When the user puts in the right answer, they are going to get the statement or message that you list out. But what happens when they make a wrong answer, or at least one that is considered false based on the conditions that you put inside the code?

There are going to be times when your user will put in an answer that is considered false based on your conditions. This doesn't mean that the user is wrong. But if you set up a program that only allows for ages that are 21 and over, the only time that your user will get a response with the if statement is when they are over the age of 21. When they answer that they are 18 or some other age that is under 21, you are going to get a blank screen.

This is not going to look very professional for your code. The user may assume that something is wrong with your program since nothing is showing up. And this is why learning about the if...else statements is so important. These are meant to provide one answer if your conditions are met, and then a second answer if the conditions are not met.

So with the example above, let's say that your program asks the user what their age is, and you are setting it up so that the answer is true only if the user is 21 or above. If the user puts in that their age is something like 25, the system will see that this is a true answer and will display your first statement. You can choose what statement you would like to show up here, such as "Congratulations, you are allowed to enter the site."

Then, instead of turning the program off, when the user places in an age that is below 21, such as 18, the program will see that this is a false answer. It will skip the first statement in your code and move on to the second statement that you put in. This message could be something like "Sorry, you must be 21 to enter this site."

You are able to add in as many of these if…else statements to your code as you would like. Sometimes it is good to separate out things into different categories. For example, say you are asking your user what their favorite animal is between cat, dog, horse, or fish. If the person says that they like cat, your program would see that answer as meeting the conditions and being true and would display the function that you have there. But if they state that fish is their favorite answer, the program would find that the three answers above were all false, and it would keep going down the line until it ran into the one that is true.

This is a pretty simple way that you will be able to add in some more options to the program. The user will be able to input the answers that they would like and you can set up the program to respond based on the answer that the user gives. While the if statements are good ones to get started with if you are not used to programming, in most cases you will want to set up the if…else statement to ensure that the program will continue on regardless of the answer that the user gives.

The Switch Statements

Another conditional statement that you may choose to use inside of your code is the switch statement. This statement is going to make it easier to test out the variables inside of your code to see the equality of them against a list of known values. A singular value in this option is going to be called a case and the variable that is switched on is going to be checked for each of the existing cases.

CHAPTER - 7
ITERATION STATEMENTS AND LOOPING STATEMENTS IN JAVA

When working with Java, you may come into situations where you must loop through a large number of numbers in the program. If we use some of the tips we have learned so far to loop through a hundred numbers, or perhaps more, we would need to use one hundred of the "if" statements from above. This is not really practical; who wants to spend all that time writing out a hundred if statements. It is messy, takes up a lot of time, makes the code harder to read, and is just not necessary.

Luckily, Java is set up to avoid some of the issues with having to write out that many if statements thanks to using loops. There are three loop types that work in Java and deciding on when depends on what you would like the code to do.

The While Loop

The first loop to look at is the while loop. This is a control structure that allows you to repeat the task as many times as you choose. Instead of having to do the if statements to count for example, you could set up the while loop to repeat the same task a hundred times. It is more efficient in space and the time it takes you to complete. The syntax to use for a while loop includes:

```
while (expression) {

// insert code

}
```

This is going to work like the if statements we debated before, but this one is set up to continue looping through the code for the entire time the expression is true. Once the expression becomes false, the code will stop looping. It is also possible for the loop to continue until the user ends it if all the conditions keep coming up true. Let's take a look at an example of how the while loop would look with some information inside:

```
int x = 10;

while (x>0)}

System.out.println(x);

x--;

}
```

For this code, the value of X is going to print out, and then it will continuously subtract one from this value until you end up with x being greater than or less than zero. If you ran this code, you are going to get an output of all the numbers from one to ten. When your x value is zero, the expression is going to return a false value, and the loop will finally end.

Watch out for infinite loops in your code. This is basically going to freeze up the program because nothing is going to end up making the loop false. It usually happens when there is some error with your logic and so the system sees that all the answers are true, therefor repeating the program over and over again.

The Do While Loop

The do while loop is going to work in a similar manner as the while loop, but there is one difference. The "do", or the part that happens when your statement is true, is going to be called before you ask the condition. This means that the do while loop is always going to run through at least one time. Rather than waiting to see if the statement is true, the do while loop will complete one loop, and then check to see if the condition is true. If it is true, it runs a second loop and so on. Once the do while loop finds that the condition is false, it will stop running.

A good example of the do while loop includes:

```
int x = 10;

do{

System.out.println(x);

x--;

while(x>0);
```

in this example, the program logic from your while look is transferred directly to the while loop. The only difference in this syntax compared to the while loop is that the logic that runs when your statements are true is going to be above the while loop, rather than below it. This output is going to be the same as with the while loop, but the following example will make some differences:

```
int x = 0;

do{

System.out.println(x)

x--;

}

while(x>0);
```

For this example, the output would be different compared to the while loop. If you wrote this out as just a while loop, the code would never run because it would end up being false in the first round. But, with the do while loop, the loop will run once, see that the statement is false, and then stop. So if you would like to make sure that the loop runs at least one time, you will need to use the syntax for the do while loop.

For Loops

For loops will help you to do increments and loops through ranges of values inside of your statement. The syntax you can use with the for loop is as follows:

```
for(initialization; termination; increment){

//statement

}
```

In this code, the initialization is going to initialize the counter variable that you would like to use. Termination will state the expression that the system should evaluate to see if it is true or false. And the increment is going to be the increments that are initialized in the counter variable. An example of how this would work with coding includes:

```
for)int x = 0; x < 10; x++){

System.out.println(x);

}
```

For this example, we start by bringing up the loop. We then create a new int that is called "x" and set it to be zero. We state when this int will terminate, saying that the loop should continue as long as x stays less than ten. We will then set the increment of increase for the x value to be by one.

The initialization is only going to occur once, right when you call the for loop. After this is initialized, it will run at least once. Once one loop is done, it is going to call the next increment value and then check to see if the program should terminate. If it doesn't get terminated, the increment value would be called again. This would continue on until the system determines that the statement is false and it is time to stop. With the code above, the loop will repeat with all the numbers from zero to nine, but will terminate when it reaches 10.

The loop statements can help to simplify your code while getting the right information to show up in the compiler. For example, the regular loop statement will help to run the program after reading the statements and determining whether the answer is true or false and then the do while loop would run the program first before checking the statements and determining if they should repeat again. These will save you a lot of time and effort and can provide the same power that you want inside your coding.

Project/Exercise

You must export a finished program if you want to run it without Eclipse or if you want to run it on a different computer.

If you export your program, it will be made into a JAR file (a Java ARchive file) on your computer. JAR files have names that end with ".jar". To run the program, double-click

on the JAR file.

Try It

1. Right-click on the *ASCII Art* project in the *Package Explorer* pane and choose *Export*.
2. Select *Runnable JAR File*, as shown in the image below, and click *Next*.
3. Select the *ASCIIArt Launch configuration,* as shown in the image below.
4. Enter *ASCIIArt.jar* for the *Export destination,* as shown in the image below.
5. Select the option to *Package required libraries into generated JAR*, as shown in this image:

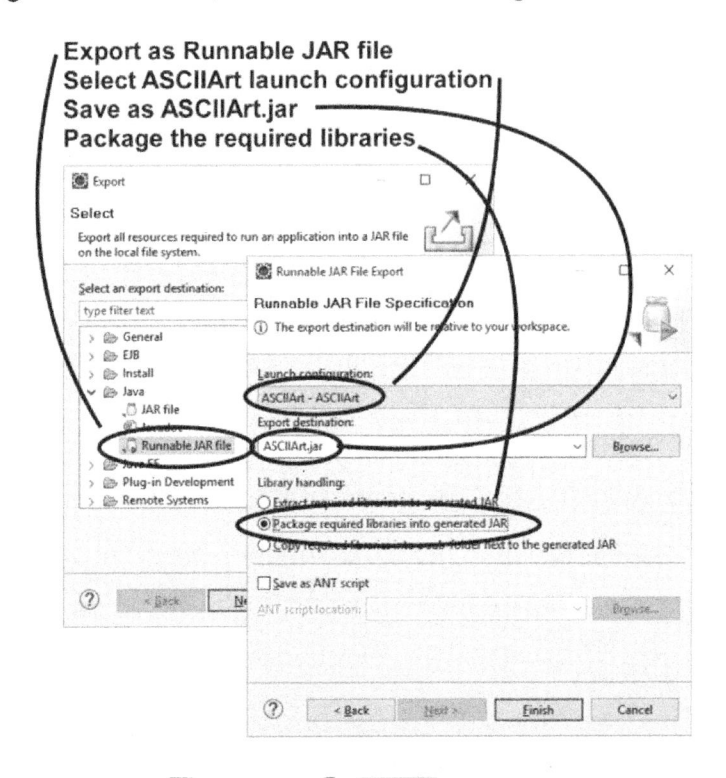

6. Click *Finish* to complete the export.

To run your program without Eclipse:

1. Find *ASCIIArt.jar* in your Java work folder.

2. Double-click *ASCIIArt.jar*.

CHAPTER - 8

CLASSES, OBJECT AND METHODS

OOP or object oriented programming is a paradigm in programming that is based on structures called objects. Using objects, programs that you write become more flexible and easier to maintain. It's like you're using a variable that can contain more than one type of data and it can contain more values. It's something dynamic that you can change. It's like a page off a record book where you can add more information, remove them, change the information, and change how the pages are organized.

OOP Concepts

To help you understand what OOP is in Java programming, we will go over what an object, class, and constructors are. We will also go over the important features of object oriented programming such as encapsulation, abstraction, polymorphism, and inheritances.

What are Objects?

Think of objects as bundles of data—a more powerful variable as it were. Now, other than bundles of data (remember, variables only hold or contain data) objects in Java also contain the actual instructions that create some sort of behavior—in other words they contain methods.

For emphasis: objects in Java programming have 2 defining characteristics. They have **states** (i.e. the bundle of data) and they have behaviors (i.e. methods). Here's a sample theoretical construction of these concepts.

Let's say we want to sell houses. In order to organize the data about the houses we have on sale we create a Java program that has objects we will call House. This object should contain every bit of information about the houses we are selling. Apart from that, some houses will get sold (account is closed) and some are still open for purchase.

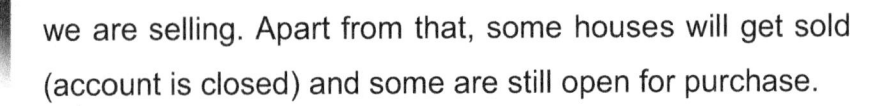

So, when we design the House object it will be something like this:

- Object name: House
- States (the data it will contain): floor area, color, address, rooms, price
- Behavior: open for sale, closed for sale

Note that some buyers may back out of a sale so even if we have closed a house for sale we should be able to open it again in case the deal doesn't get completed. We want the action to come from the object itself so that each house object that we create can stand on its own.

Now if we had to write an object in Java code that had all those details including the behaviors and states mentioned in that description above, then it might look something like this:

```
class House {
    String address;
    String color;
    double are;
    void openDoor() {
        //Write code here
    }
    void closeDoor() {
        //Write code here
    }
    ...
    ...
}
```

Now, if you notice in the example above we are introducing another Java programming structure called a *class*. We'll go over what a class is and other details but we just have to go over a few more details about objects first.

Characteristics of Objects

There are three main characteristics of objects that you should know about, which include the following:

1. Abstraction
2. Encapsulation
3. Message passing

Abstraction simply refers to the process of hiding unnecessary details of an object and only showing the ones that are relevant. **Encapsulation** on the other hand simply means the binding of the states and the methods of an object together.

This binding eventually creates something called a class (we'll cover that in a little bit). Finally, **message passing** refers to the ability of objects to interact with other objects.

What are Classes in Java OOP?

As you can see in the sample code earlier (i.e. line 1) that defined the object called House, it began by declaring something called a Class using this line:

Class House {

So, what is a class in object oriented programming? Think of it as a blueprint that you will use to create objects. The first step to creating an object is to declare or define what needs to be in it and you do that by using classes.

Here's another example of a class in Java:

```
1   public class Dog {
2       String breed;
3       int age;
4       String color;
5
6       void barking() {
7       }
8
9       void hungry() {
10      }
11
12      void sleeping() {
13      }
14  }
```

In this example the states in this class, which is called Dog, are breed, age, and color, which you can find in lines 2 to 4. And the behavior or methods contained in it include barking, hungry, and sleeping.

As you can see in our examples above, blueprints or *Classes* can also contain variables (i.e. primitive variables). However, do take note that there are three different types of variables that can exist inside a class in Java. They include the following:

1. **Local Variables** – local variables only function within a method. Once all the lines in that method have been executed the local variables in it get discarded. They can't be used elsewhere in your source code or even in your entire program.
2. **Instance Variables** – instance variables are the variables that can be found within a class but are found outside of a method. Note that methods that are inside the class can use instance variables in that class.
3. **Class Variables** – these are variables that are also inside a class and also outside any method within that class. The big difference is that class variables are created using the static keyword.

Remember that you can add as many methods inside a class as you need. You can also have these methods access the other methods within the same class. And when you finally create an object using the class that you have designed or written then that object is called an *instance* of that class.

What are Constructors?

This is another important topic in Java OOP. A constructor in Java is a specialized method that you will use to initialize an object. But what if you forget to write a constructor? If that happens, then the compiler will create a constructor for you.

Every time you create an object it should have a constructor. At least one constructor will be invoked for every object that you create using a class—at least. That means a class or object can have more than one constructor. Note that constructors should have the same name as the class.

Here is an example of a source code that has a constructor in it:

```
1   public class Puppy {
2       public Puppy() {
3       }
4
5       public Puppy(String name) {
6           // This is the constructor
7       }
8   }
```

The constructor in this example is found on line 5.

How to Create an Object in Java

Now we are ready to create an object in Java. Remember that you create an object in using the Classes (i.e. the blueprints) that you have defined in your source code. Write the class first and then create the object after. Well, to be exact, there are three steps in order to create an object in Java.

1. Make a declaration including the name for the type of object that you want to create.

2. Create an instance (i.e. an actual object based on the class that you wrote) using the keyword "new".
3. Use a call to a constructor to initialize the new object that has just been created.

Here is an example of a program that creates an object using the steps mentioned above:

```
public class Puppy {
    public Puppy(String name) {
        // This constructor has one parameter, name.
        System.out.println("Passed Name is :" + name );
    }

    public static void main(String []args) {
        // Following statement would create an object myPuppy
        Puppy myPuppy = new Puppy( "Fido" );
    }
}
```

Running and compiling that program will print the following output to the screen:

Passed Name is : Fido

Note that when the actual instance of that class (i.e. the object) is created (line 9) it is then initialized by the constructor that was defined on line 4.

Using Methods and Variables within Objects

The methods and variables that can be found inside an instance can be accessed through the objects themselves. Here are the steps to access methods and variables via an object:

1. Create an object by using an object reference and a new constructor. You will use the following syntax:

   "ObjectReference = new Constructor();"

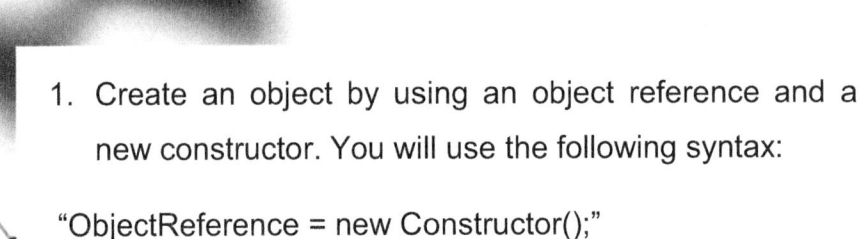

   where *ObjectReference* is the name of the object.

2. Call a variable within the object using the following syntax:

   ObjectReference.variableName;

3. Call a class method using the following syntax:

   ObjectReference.MethodName();

   Let's go over a sample program that will help us walk through the said steps:

```
1   public class Puppy {
2       int puppyAge;
3
4       public Puppy(String name) {
5           // This constructor has one parameter, name.
6           System.out.println("Name chosen is :" + name );
7       }
8
9       public void setAge( int age ) {
10          puppyAge = age;
11      }
12
13      public int getAge( ) {
14          System.out.println("Puppy's age is :" + puppyAge );
15          return puppyAge;
16      }
17
18      public static void main(String []args) {
19          /* Object creation */
20          Puppy myPuppy = new Puppy( "tommy" );
21
22          /* Call class method to set puppy's age */
23          myPuppy.setAge( 2 );
24
25          /* Call another class method to get puppy's age */
26          myPuppy.getAge( );
27
28          /* You can access instance variable as follows as well */
29          System.out.println("Variable Value :" + myPuppy.puppyAge );
30      }
31  }
```

The class declaration is as follows: "public class Puppy" which creates the class called Puppy. It has an int class variable called puppyAge (line 2).

It is followed by the constructor on line 4 that prints out to the screen. Note also that this class/object will have 2 behaviors or methods. The first one is called setAge( ) which assigns the age of the puppy. This is the first class method.

Note line 10. The class variable puppyAge will be set to the same or equal value of the parameter for the method setAge. The second class method is called getAge( ), which returns the age of the puppy.

The main program starts at line 18. The new object or instance of the class Puppy is created using this line:

Puppy myPuppy = new Puppy("tommy");

The name of the object is myPuppy and the constructor initializes the name to "tommy".

The value of the class variable puppyAge is then set to 2 using the statement on line 23 that goes:

myPuppy.setAge(2);

Programming Tip: Remember, to access a method within an object follow this format:

<name of object>.<name of method> (<object parameters>)

You can also access the variables inside an instance using the syntax described above.

CHAPTER - 9
ADVANCED OBJECT ORIENTED PROGRAMMING

Object-Oriented Programming (OOPs) is the guiding concept of the Java language. Knowledge of OOPs and its core principles is useful in the process of learning and understanding Java. OOPs entails organizing programs on the basis of data parameters, such that instructions provide the definition of data and specifies the manipulations to be performed on the data. This part provides a detailed discussion of the four core characteristics of OOPs including encapsulation, polymorphism, inheritance, and data abstraction.

Encapsulation

Encapsulation in Java programming involves the establishment of links between codes and data. The encapsulation process creates a chain between codes and the data that has been designated for manipulation. The OOPs environment provides the infrastructure for linking codes and data into unitary units. This process culminates in the creation of a black box containing wrapped codes and data. The transformation of code and data into a linked format actually forms an object which acts as a supporting platform for encapsulation. The object is tuned to operate on the default code or alternatively change the settings for accessing data to either a private or public state. A private default setting restricts code or data accessibility to another program within the object. A public default setting, on the other hand, allows access by programs that are external to the object. The public access programs act as channels for interacting with the private programs in the object.

```
public class Encapsulate{
```

```
//private variable declaration

//access restricted to

//public class methods

private String carName;

private int carVin;

//get method for vin to facilitate accessibility

//private variable carVin

public int getVin()

{

return carVin;

}

//get method for name to facilitate accessibility

//private variable carName

public String getName()

{

return carName;

}

//set method for name to facilitate accessibility

//private variable carVin
```

```java
public void setVin(int newVin)

{

carVin = newVin;

}

//set method for name to facilitate accessibility

//private variable carName

public void setName(String newName)

{

carName = newName;

}

}
```

The example above compiles in Javac but generates an error if you run it in Java. The reason behind this discrepancy is because the code does not contain the main method declaration to generate a coding outcome for the Java program. The encapsulation process requires the compilation of additional parameters that will provide the getter and setter methods for accessing individual classes in the program. The setter and getter methods for this particular example would appear like the one below.

```java
public class TestingEncapsulate{

public static void main(String args[]){

Encapsulate itm = new Encapsulate();

itm.setName("Ford");

itm.setVin(123123);

System.out.println(" car Name: " + itm.getName());

System.out.println("car Vin: " + itm.getVin());

}

}
```

Note that this particular segment has a main method declaration and its class name has been changed to TestingEncapsulate. However, this segment cannot compile or run on its own. It must be joined to the first segment so that it can complete the circuit of the setter and getter methods for accessing the private data. As such, we will copy/paste the second segment on top of the javac-compiled Encapsulate.java file to introduce the main class declaration. Copy/pasting it at the bottom would generate an error message and fail to compile. It is equally important to note that although we will have TestingEncapsulate at the top alongside the main method declaration, the javac-compiled file will retain the Encapsulate.java name.

```java
public class TestingEncapsulate{

public static void main(String args[]){

Encapsulate itm = new Encapsulate();

itm.setName("Ford");

itm.setVin(123123);

System.out.println(" car Name: " + itm.getName());

System.out.println("car Vin: " + itm.getVin());

}

}

public class Encapsulate{

//private variable declaration

//access restricted to

//public class methods

private String carName;

private int carVin;

//get method for vin to facilitate accessibility

//private variable carVin
```

```java
public int getVin()

{

return carVin;

}

//get method for name to facilitate accessibility

//private variable carName

public String getName()

{

return carName;

}

//set method for name to facilitate accessibility

//private variable carVin

public void setVin(int newVin)

{

carVin = newVin;

}

//set method for name to facilitate accessibility

//private variable carName

public void setName(String newName)
```

```
{
carName = newName;
}
}
```

The output for the code will be as follows.

car Name: Ford

car Vin: 123123

Objects and Classes

The use of objects and classes to implement encapsulation is meant to create secure and controlled operations in single units of programming. Since Java is essentially an object-driven programming language and platform, these objects are real life items like cars or books that can be quantified using values, digits, or counts. The only exceptions for deviating from the quantitative reference to objects in Java occur when using the primitive-type parameters to describe data. Since objects are derived from classes, particular types of objects bear similar properties to the particular class from which they were generated.

The class carries the properties or declarations that describe the characteristics of particular types of objects. There are different types of classes and some of them can be used in the development of real-time software solutions. These classes could be anonymous, nested, or any other types that are designed for use in Java programming. A class has within it several elements including modifiers, class name, and body, among others. The modifier describes whether a class is accessible publicly or not. If the access is not public, it provides default private access declaration. The Class name component requires that initial letters be capitalized when labeling classes. The body component specifies that a class name must be positioned inside opening and closing braces like {}.

Inheritance in Java

In Java programming, main classes are capable of transferring their traits to subsidiary ones through a process known as inheritance. The subsidiary, or baby, classes usually bear similar traits to those of the parent classes. Such processes that recreate classes are crucial in application development because they facilitate the creation of new class categories. The process of replicating class traits also provides the convenience of manipulating, expanding, and redeploying the methods and fields that reside in the preferred classes.

The newly created classes are not one-hundred percent similar to the parent class. Each class has its own unique attributes and the inheritance process only serves to transfer the shared traits. This simplifies coding for developers because they avoid the duplication of shared class traits and concentrate on the development of unique traits when creating subclasses. The syntax structure best demonstrates the nature of the transfer of the data profile of the members and methods of a class from the main class to the subclass. The word 'extends' is inserted in the code to show that a subclass is more or less a continuation of the main class. For example, if Bee is the subclass being created from Hive, then it would simply be expressed as 'Bee extends Hive'.

```
class Transport{

void commute() {System.out.println("commuting");}

}

class Train extends Transport{

void city() {System.out.println("intercity");}

}
```

```
class InheritanceSampling{

public static void main(String args[]){

Train t=new Train();

t.city();

t.commute();

}

}
```

Run the program above in Javac to compile and create its class. If you run the program in Java, it will generate a "can't find main(String[]) method in class" error. To run the code successfully in Java, — that is, java filename.java — transfer the block of the code containing the main(String[]) method to the top section.

```
public static void main(String args[]){

Train t=new Train();

t.city();

t.commute();

}

}

class Transport{
```

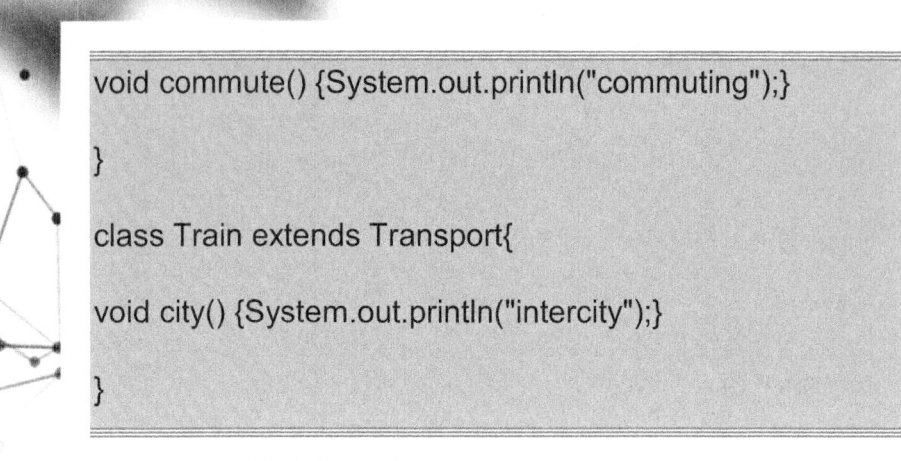

```
void commute() {System.out.println("commuting");}

}

class Train extends Transport{

void city() {System.out.println("intercity");}

}
```

The code will deliver the outcome below.

intercity

commuting

The inheritance of traits between the main and subclass is subject to limitations when the members or methods in question are declared as private. The direct transfer of traits is restricted to the public members or methods within a class. Indirect paths have to be used to open up the private attributes of the parent class to the subsidiary class. In fact, access to the private traits of the main class by the subclass is only possible through the use of protected methods residing in the former. But this type of inheritance does not expose the private data members or methods beyond the subclass. The acquired protected traits become accessible to only the sub and the parent class.

Multilevel inheritance prevails when the subclass exists as an extension of the main class. It occurs in a linear structure whereby the parent class shares its traits to a chain of offshoots. In other words, the main class passes its characteristics to the subclass, which in turn shares the attributes to its offshoot, and so on. Just like a family or genealogy tree, this chain can stretch and spread out to an extent where the class at the top of the chain would become the ancestor class.

```
class Transport{
void commute() {System.out.println("commuting");}
}
class Train extends Transport{
void city() {System.out.println("intercity");}
}
class Ticket extends Train{
void discount() {System.out.println("discounting");}
}
class InheritanceSampling{
public static void main(String args[]){
Ticket t=new Ticket();
```

```
t.discount();

t.city();

t.commute();

   }

}
```

Project

A switch statement lets you run a different block of code for each expected value of a variable.

Try It

Ask the user what to do.

1. Ask for input from the user, and put his/her answer into a string called choice.

Listing 6-4, from ChooseAnAdventure.java

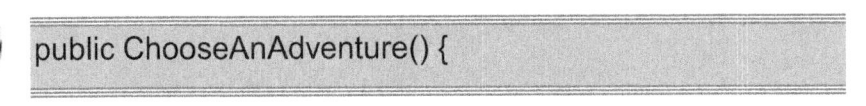

...

```
public ChooseAnAdventure() {
```

...

```
print("c) Plant the beans?");

String _____ = _____;
```

Completed listing

You could write a long if statement to check if choice is equal to "a", else if choice is equal to "b", else if choice is equal to "c". However, there's another type of code that checks if a value is equal to one of several choices. It's called a switch statement.

The usual switch statement looks like this:

```
switch(_____) {

case _____ :

   _____;

   _____;

   break;

case _____ :

   _____;

   _____;

   break;

case _____ :

   _____;

   _____;
```

```
    break;
}
```

To fill in the details of the switch statement:

- switch - put the variable to be checked for the different values in the parentheses. For example, if you want to check if the variable reply is "Yes" or "No", use:
- switch(reply) {
- case - create one case and its value for each expected value. For example, if one of the expected values is "Yes", use:
- case "Yes" :
- : - place one or more lines of code after the colon to be run when the variable has the value of that case.
- break; - put a break statement at the end of the code for the case. The program will then skip to the end of the switch statement.

1. Add a switch statement to:
   a. Print "Going up the hill." if the user enters "a".
   b. Print "Checking the cottage." if the user enters "b".
   c. Print "Planting beans." if the user enters "c".

Listing 6-5, from ChooseAnAdventure.java

...

```
public ChooseAnAdventure() {

    ...

    String choice = input();

    switch(choice) {

    case "___" :

      print("_____");

      break;

    case "___" :

      print("_____");

      break;

    case "___" :

      print("_____");

      break;

    }

    ...
```

Completed listing

CHAPTER - 10
COLLECTIONS

The Java Collections Framework is a lot of pre-composed classes and interfaces that Java gives to assist us with arranging and control gatherings of articles. Utilizing the Collections Framework, we can decide to sort out our articles in various arrangements, for example, records, sets, lines or guides.

We'll be seeing how to utilize records in this part.

The Java Collections Framework normalizes the manner by which gatherings of articles are taken care of. Henceforth, when you realize how to utilize records, you'll see it simpler to learn different assortments, for example, sets or lines.

Autoboxing and Unboxing

Before we can examine the Java Collections Framework, we have to initially talk about the idea of autoboxing and unpacking.

We found out about the 8 crude sorts in Java. These 8 crude sorts are fundamental information types and not objects.

Be that as it may, Java is an item arranged language and a lot of language rotates around regarding everything as an article. Thus, as a rule, we think that its important to change over a crude sort into an article.

To encourage this transformation, Java gives us what is known as covering classes. Every crude sort in Java has a comparing covering class. These covering classes contain various helpful strategies that we can utilize. The covering classes for boolean, singe, byte, short, int, long, buoy and twofold are Boolean, Character, Byte, Short, Integer, Long, Float and Double individually.

Changing over from a crude information type into a covering class object is simple.

For example, to change over int into an Integer object, we do the accompanying:

Whole number intObject = new Integer(100);

Here, we announce and start up an Integer object by passing an int estimation of 100 to the Integer class constructor. This constructor acknowledges the worth and makes an Integer object dependent on that esteem.

On the off chance that we need to change over the Integer object back to an int, we utilize the intValue() technique. The code is as per the following:

```
int m = intObject.intValue();
```

The intValue() strategy restores an int type which we allocate to m.

As should be obvious, changing over from a crude information type to an item and the other way around is moderately clear. Anyway practically speaking, it is really easier than what is appeared formerly. Java gives us two systems known as autoboxing and unpacking. This takes into consideration programmed transformation.

To change over from int to Integer, rather than composing

```
Whole number intObject = new Integer(100);
```

We can essentially compose

```
Whole number intObject = 100;
```

Here, we essentially allocate the worth 100 to intObject. We don't have to pass this int incentive to the Integer constructor; Java does it for us behind the scene. This procedure is known as autoboxing.

To change over from Integer to int, rather than composing

```
int m = intObject.intValue();
```

We can basically compose

```
int m = intObject;
```

We don't have to expressly utilize the intValue() technique. At the point when we dole out an Integer article to an int variable, Java consequently changes over the Integer item to int type. This procedure is known as unpacking.

As should be obvious, covering classes give us a helpful method to change over crude kinds into articles and bad habit refrain. Other than this reason, covering classes likewise have another significant use – they give us techniques for changing over strings into crude sorts. Assume you need to change over a string into an int, you can utilize the parseInt() technique in the Integer class as demonstrated as follows:

```
int n = Integer.parseInt("5");
```

Note that "5" is a string as we utilize twofold statements. The Integer.parseInt("5") strategy restores the int esteem 5, which we at that point relegate to n.

In the event that the string can't be changed over into an int, the strategy will toss a NumberFormatException. For example, the announcement underneath will give us a blunder:

```
int p = Integer.parseInt("ABC");
```

Notwithstanding changing over a string into an int, we can likewise change over a string into a twofold utilizing the parseDouble() strategy found in the Double class:

```
Twofold q = Double.parseDouble("5.1");
```

Likewise, we'll get a blunder if the string can't be changed over into a twofold.

Lists

Since we know about covering classes, let us take a gander at records. A rundown is fundamentally the same as an exhibit, yet is increasingly adaptable. In particular, its size can be changed.

We discovered that the size of an exhibit can't be changed once we instate the cluster or on the off chance that we express the quantity of components while proclaiming it.

For example, on the off chance that you announce the cluster as

```
int[] myArray = new int[10];
```

Myarray can just hold 10 qualities. On the off chance that you compose myArray[10] (which alludes to the eleventh incentive since cluster list begins from zero), you will get a mistake.

On the off chance that you need more prominent adaptability in your program, you can utilize a rundown. Java accompanies a pre-composed List interface that is a piece of the Java Collections Framework. This interface is executed by a couple of classes. The most normally utilized classes that execute the List interface are the ArrayList and LinkedList classes. We'll take a gander at ArrayList first.

ArrayList

The ArrayList class is a pre-composed class that actualizes the List interface. Like every single other assortment in the Java Collections Framework, an ArrayList must be utilized to store objects (not crude information types). Consequently, in the event that we need to pronounce a rundown of numbers, we need to utilize Integer rather than int.

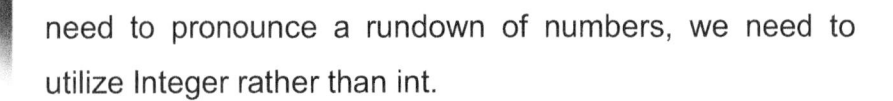

At whatever point you utilize an ArrayList, you need to import the java.util.ArrayList class utilizing the announcement beneath

Import java.util.ArrayList;

The sentence structure for pronouncing and launching an ArrayList is as per the following:

```
ArrayList<Type> nameOfArrayList = new ArrayList<>();
```

For example, to announce and start up an ArrayList of Integer objects, we compose

```
ArrayList<Integer> userAgeList = new ArrayList<>();
```

On the left half of the announcement, we pronounced an ArrayList variable.

ArrayList is a watchword to demonstrate that you are announcing an ArrayList

<Integer> shows that this ArrayList is utilized to store Integer objects

userAgeList is the name of the ArrayList.

On the correct side, we start up another ArrayList object utilizing the new watchword and allocate it to userAgeList.

On the off chance that you need the ArrayList to store String objects rather, you announce and start up it as

```
ArrayList<String> userNameList = new ArrayList<>();
```

In the two models above, we explicitly proclaimed an ArrayList and doled out an ArrayList to it. In any case, in the event that you like, you can likewise decide to proclaim a List rather and dole out an ArrayList to it.

This is permitted in light of the fact that List is the superinterface of ArrayList.

To announce a List and appoint an ArrayList to it, we compose

```
List<String> userNameList2 = new ArrayList<>();
```

You have to import java.util.List in the event that you do it thusly.

ArrayList Methods

The ArrayList class accompanies countless pre-composed techniques that we can utilize. All strategies talked about underneath can be utilized whether you proclaimed an ArrayList or you announced a List and appointed an ArrayList to it.

```
include()
```

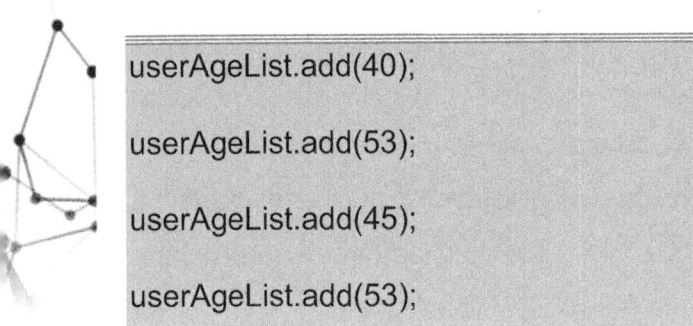

To add individuals to a rundown, utilize the include() strategy.

```
userAgeList.add(40);

userAgeList.add(53);

userAgeList.add(45);

userAgeList.add(53);
```

userAgeList currently has 4 individuals.

You can utilize System.out.println() to print out the individuals from a rundown. On the off chance that you compose

```
System.out.println(userAgeList);
```

you'll get

[40, 53, 45, 53]

as the yield.

To include individuals at a particular position, do the accompanying:

```
userAgeList.add(2, 51);

This embeds the number 51 into file 2 (for example the third position).
```

userAgeList currently becomes [40, 53, 51, 45, 53].

set()

To supplant a component at a predefined position with another component, utilize the set() strategy.

For example, to change the component at list 3 to 49, do the accompanying:

userAgeList.set(3, 49);

The primary contention is the list of the component that you need to supplant and the subsequent contention is the worth that you need to supplant it with.

userAgeList currently becomes [40, 53, 51, 49, 53].

evacuate()

To evacuate part at a particular situation from the rundown, utilize the expel() strategy. The evacuate() strategy takes in the record of the thing to be expelled as contention. For example, on the off chance that we compose

userAgeList.remove(3);

The component at list 3 is expelled.

userAgeList becomes [40, 53, 51, 53].

get()

To get the component at a particular position, utilize the get() technique.

```
userAgeList.get(2);
```

gives us the number 51.

size()

To discover the quantity of components in the rundown, utilize the size() strategy.

userAgeList.size() gives us 4 as there are 4 components in the ArrayList right now.

contains()

To check if a rundown contains a specific part, utilize the contains() technique.

To check if userAgeList contains '51', we compose

```
userAgeList.contains(51);
```

we will get valid as the outcome.

On the off chance that we compose

```
userAgeList.contains(12);
```

we will get bogus as the outcome.

indexOf()

To get the record of the primary event of a specific component, utilize the indexOf() technique. In the event that the component doesn't exist in the ArrayList, the technique returns - 1.

For example, in the event that we compose

```
userAgeList.indexOf(53);
```

we'll get 1 as the outcome. Despite the fact that 53 shows up in the ArrayList twice, we'll just get the list of the main event.

In the event that we compose

```
userAgeList.indexOf(12);
```

we'll get - 1 as the number 12 doesn't exist in the ArrayList.

toArray()

To get all the components in the ArrayList, utilize the toArray() strategy. This strategy restores a variety of Object type containing the entirety of the components in the ArrayList in legitimate succession (from first to last component).

For example, we can compose

```
Object[] myArray = userAgeList.toArray();
```

to change over userAgeList to an Object[] cluster. (Review that the Object class is the parent class of all classes in J

LinkedList

A LinkedList is fundamentally the same as an ArrayList and is consequently fundamentally the same as use. The two of them execute the List interface.

The primary distinction between a LinkedList and an ArrayList is their usage. An ArrayList is executed as a resizable cluster. As more components are included, its size is expanded powerfully. At whatever point we add another component to the center of an ArrayList, all the components after it must be moved. For example, if myArrayList has three components as demonstrated as follows

```
myArrayList = {"Hello", "Great", "Morning"};
```

what's more, we need to embed the string "Scene" into position 1 (for example after "Hi"), all the components after "Hi" must be moved.

Also, when we erase a component from an ArrayList, all the components after the erased component must be moved up. This can bring about a critical postponement if the ArrayList is enormous.

In the event that there is a requirement for visit expansion and erasure of components from a List, it is smarter to utilize a LinkedList. A LinkedList stores the addresses of the components when every component. For example, assume a LinkedList has three components "Hi", "Great" and "Morning" at addresses 111, 122 and 133 individually. The chart beneath shows how a LinkedList is executed.

As "Hi" is the primary component, there is no component before it. Subsequently the container on the left shows a bolt highlighting (invalid essentially implies it is highlighting nothing). The crate on the correct stores the location 122, which is the location of the following component.

For the component "Great", the crate on the left stores the location 111 (the location of the past component) and the container on the correct stores the location 133 (the location of the following component).

Presently assume we erase the component "Great". The chart underneath shows how the addresses are refreshed (the underlined addresses).

For the component "Hi", the case on the correct presently stores the location 133, which is the location of the component "Morning".

At the point when the List is actualized in that capacity, there is no compelling reason to move any component when components are included or erased. The addresses are essentially refreshed when important

Since there is currently no component highlighting the component "Great", the Java Virtual Machine will in the long run erase this component in order to let loose any memory that it might be utilizing.

When to utilize a LinkedList over an ArrayList?

For the most part, we utilize a LinkedList when there is a need to include or evacuate components much of the time.

Likewise, the LinkedList class executes the Queue and Deque interfaces on head of the List interface. Line and Deque are two different interfaces in the Java Collections Framework. Henceforth, you should utilize a LinkedList rather than an ArrayList on the off chance that you need to utilize any of the techniques from these two interfaces, (for example, offer(), look(), survey(), getFirst(), getLast() and so forth).

In any case, note that a LinkedList has higher memory utilization than an ArrayList as memory is expected to store the addresses of the neighboring components. It is likewise additional tedious to locate a particular component in a LinkedList as you need to begin from the principal component in the rundown and follow the references until you get to that thing. This is as opposed to an ArrayList where the location of every component can be determined dependent on the location of the main component. In this manner, it isn't fitting to utilize a LinkedList if memory is a worry or if there is a regular need to look for a component.

Presently, how about we take a gander at how we can proclaim and launch a LinkedList. The language structure is as per the following:

```
LinkedList<Type>    nameOfLinkedList    =    new LinkedList<>();
```

For example, to proclaim and launch a LinkedList of Integer objects, we compose

```
LinkedList<Integer>    userAgeLinkedList    =    new LinkedList<>();
```

This is fundamentally the same as how you proclaim and start up an ArrayList. The main contrast is you change the word ArrayList to LinkedList. You have to import the LinkedList class when utilizing a LinkedList. To do as such, utilize the import proclamation underneath:

```
import java.util.LinkedList;
```

Like an ArrayList, you can likewise decide to announce a List and dole out a LinkedList to it. To do that, you compose

```
List<Integer> userAgeLinkedList2 = new LinkedList<>();
```

On the off chance that you do it along these lines, you have to import the List class as well.

LinkedList Methods

The LinkedList class accompanies an enormous number of pre-composed techniques that we can utilize. In any case, as both the LinkedList and ArrayList classes execute the List interface, they share a great deal of similar techniques. Truth be told, all the techniques canvassed in the ArrayList area can be utilized with a LinkedList.

That implies you can utilize the include(), set(), get(), size(), evacuate(), contains(), indexOf(), toArray() and clear() strategies similarly for both ArrayList and LinkedList. To welcome this reality, dispatch NetBeans and start another Project called ListDemo.

Supplant the code with the code underneath:

```
bundle listdemo;

Introduce java.util.ArrayList;

Introduce t java.util.LinkedList;
```

```
Introduce java.util.List;

open class ListDemo {

open static void main(String[] args) {

List<Integer> userAgeList = new ArrayList<>();

userAgeList.add(40);

userAgeList.add(53);

userAgeList.add(45);

userAgeList.add(53);

userAgeList.add(2, 51);

System.out.println(userAgeList.size());

userAgeList.remove(3);

System.out.println(userAgeList.contains(12));

System.out.println(userAgeList.indexOf(12));

System.out.println(userAgeList.get(2));

Integer[] userAgeArray = userAgeList.toArray(new Integer[0]);

System.out.println(userAgeArray[0]);

System.out.println(userAgeList);

}
```

}

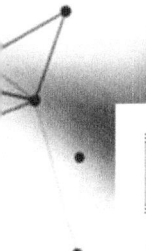

This code shows a portion of the techniques referenced in the ArrayList segment. On the off chance that you run the code, you'll get

5

False

- 1

51

40

[40, 53, 51, 53]

Presently, change the announcement

```
List<Integer> userAgeList = new ArrayList<>();
```

to

```
List<Integer> userAgeList = new LinkedList<>();
```

also, run the program once more.

What do you notice? Everything runs impeccably and you get a similar yield right?

That is on the grounds that both the ArrayList class and LinkedList class execute the List interface. Consequently a great deal of techniques are regular to the two classes.

Nonetheless, as referenced above, notwithstanding executing the List interface, the LinkedList class likewise actualizes the Queue and Deque interface. Along these lines, it has some extra techniques that are absent in the List interface and the ArrayList class.

On the off chance that you need to utilize these strategies, you need to explicitly announce a LinkedList rather than a List. Change the announcement

List<Integer> userAgeList = new LinkedList<>();

to

LinkedList<Integer> userAgeList = new LinkedList<>();

to attempt the strategies underneath.

survey()

The survey() strategy restores the principal component (otherwise called the top) of the rundown and expels the component from the rundown. It returns invalid if the rundown is unfilled.

In the event that userAgeList is right now [40, 53, 51, 53] and you compose

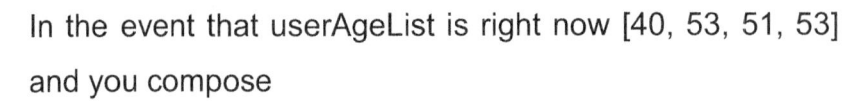

```
System.out.println(userAgeList.poll());
```

you'll get

```
40
```

as the yield since the main component in userAgeList is 40. In the event that you print out the components of the userAgeList once more, you'll get

```
[53, 51, 53].
```

The principal component is expelled from the rundown.

```
look()
```

The look() technique is like the survey() strategy. It restores the principal component of the rundown however doesn't expel the component from the rundown. It returns invalid if the rundown is vacant.

```
getFirst()
```

The getFirst() strategy is practically indistinguishable from the look() technique. It restores the primary component of the rundown and doesn't evacuate the component.

Nonetheless, it gives a NoSuchElementException special case when the rundown is vacant.

getLast()

The getLast() strategy restores the last component of the rundown and doesn't evacuate the component. It gives a NoSuchElementException special case when the rundown is unfilled.

For a total rundown of all the LinkedList strategies accessible in Java, look at this page https://docs.oracle.com/javase/8/docs/programming interface/java/util/LinkedList.html

Using Lists in our Methods

Since we know about two of the most normally utilized records in Java, let us take a gander at how we can utilize these rundowns in our techniques. Utilizing records in our techniques is fundamentally the same as how we use exhibits in our strategies. In the models underneath, we'll utilize an ArrayList of Integer articles to illustrate. A similar punctuation applies for different kinds of assortments.

To acknowledge an ArrayList<Integer> as a boundary, we pronounce the strategy as

open void methodOne(ArrayList<Integer> m)

```
{
/Some usage code
}
```

To restore an ArrayList<Integer> from a technique, we pronounce the strategy as

```
open ArrayList<Integer> methodTwo()
{
ArrayList<Integer> a = new ArrayList<>();
/Some usage code
return a;
}
```

Assume both methodOne() and methodTwo() are in a class called MyClass and

```
MyClass mc = new MyClass();
```

To call methodOne(), we go in an ArrayList as contention

```
ArrayList<Integer> b = new ArrayList<>();
```

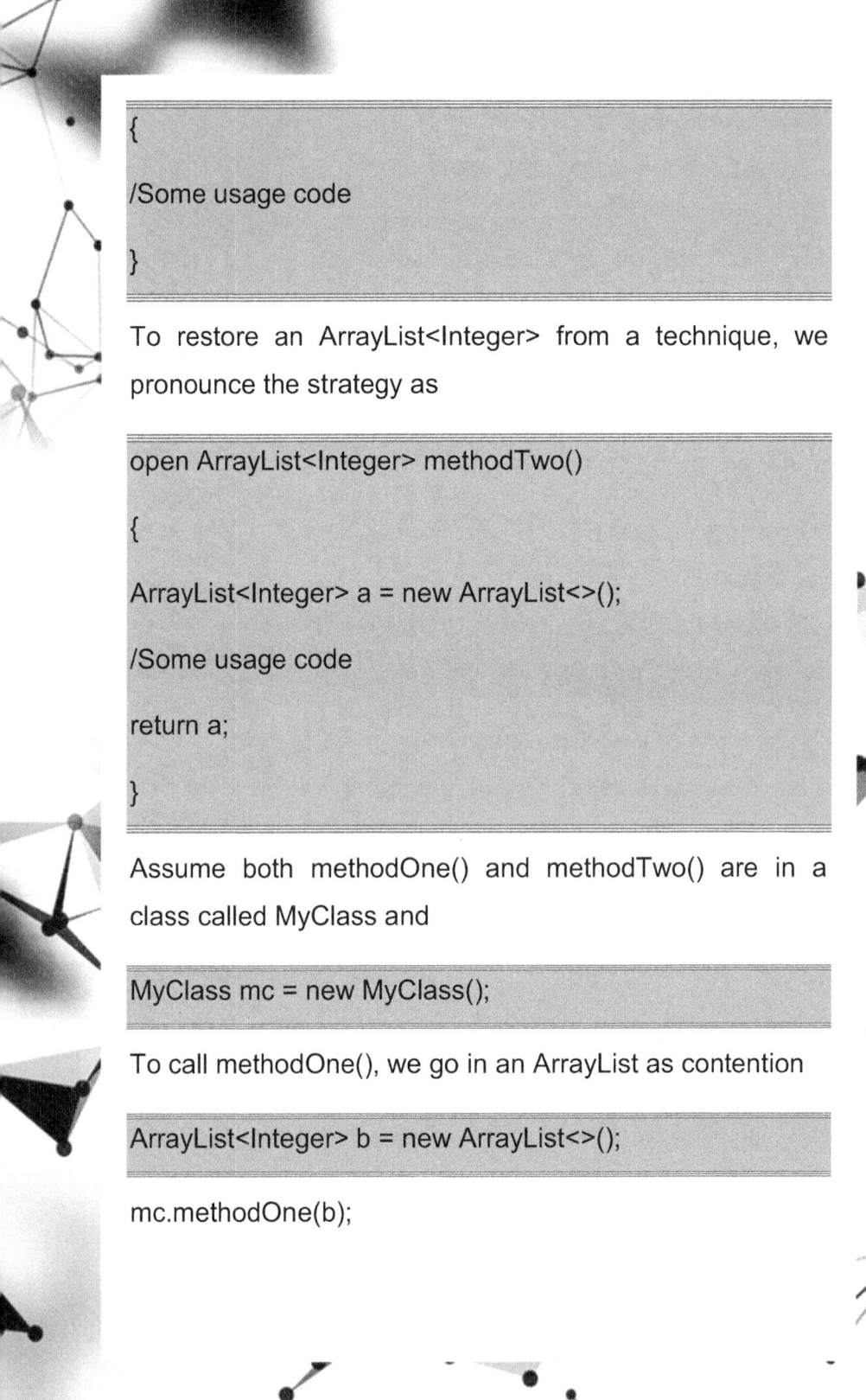

mc.methodOne(b);

To call methodTwo(), we doleced out the outcome to an ArrayList.

```
ArrayList<Integer> c = mc.methodTwo();
```

Project

Comments are notes you can put in a program to remind yourself of what you wanted the code to do. Comments are ignored when the program runs, so you can type anything you want in the comments. Comments are also often used to label parts of code.

In this lesson, you'll use comments to plan the code to scramble a word.

Try It

Start writing the next program:

1. Create a new Java project called Word Scramble and add My Window and DIYJava.jar to the project.
2. Create a new package called _____._____.wordscramble in the project.
3. Create a new class called WordScramble, with superclass MyWindow and with a stub for main() and its constructors.
4. Add code to main() to call the WordScramble constructor.

139

Listing 12-1, from WordScramble.java

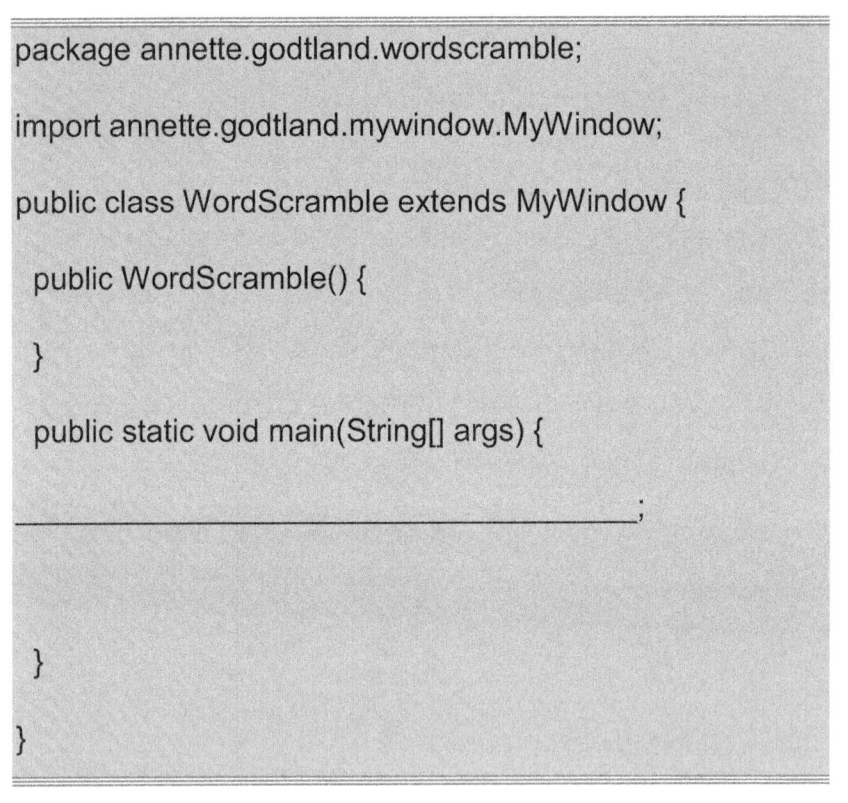

```
package annette.godtland.wordscramble;

import annette.godtland.mywindow.MyWindow;

public class WordScramble extends MyWindow {

  public WordScramble() {

  }

  public static void main(String[] args) {

    _____;



  }

}
```

Completed listing

Put the code to scramble a string in its own method so it can be used more than once.

1. Define a private method called scramble() that takes one parameter, a string called word, and returns a string.
2. In scramble(), declare a string called scrambled, assign it an initial value of an empty string, and return that string.

Listing 12-2, from WordScramble.java

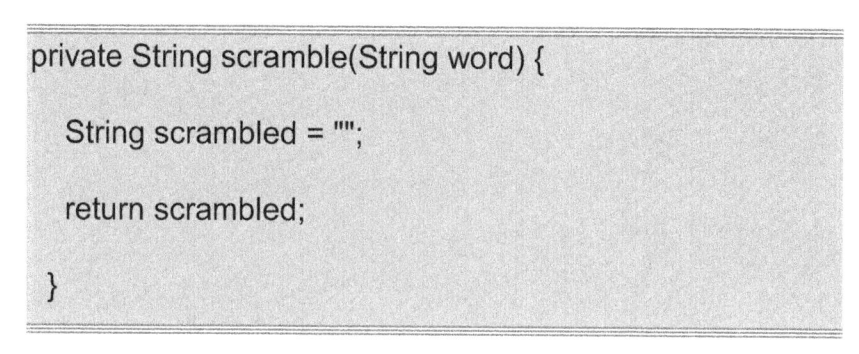

```java
private String scramble(String word) {

    String scrambled = "";

    return scrambled;

}
```

Completed listing

Add code to the constructor:

1. Create a string called word with a value of "ANIMALS".
2. Call the scramble() method with word as its parameter and assign the results of that call to a new string called scrambled.
3. Print that new string.

Listing 12-3, from WordScramble.java

...

```java
public WordScramble()

{

String word = "_____";

    String _____ = scramble(word);

    print(_____);
```

141

```
}
```

...

Completed listing

Do you know how to scramble a word? It's easier if you make it into smaller steps. To scramble a word:

- Pick a random letter from the original word.
- Remove that letter from the original word.
- Add that letter to a new word.
- Repeat these steps until all letters have been removed from the original word.

To type comments into code, start the line with two forward slashes, //. Anything you type after the // on that line is a comment.

1. Type comments in scramble() to describe the steps to scramble a word.

Listing 12-4, from WordScramble.java

...

```
private String scramble(String word) {
    String scrambled = "";
```

// pick a random letter from the original word

// remove that letter from the original word

// _____

// _____

return scrambled;

}

...

CHAPTER - 11

FILE HANDLING

What is File Handling?

Like almost any modern programming language, Java is dependent on modules and libraries to expand its capacity and capabilities. In fact, one of the first lines in almost any Java program is referencing the requisite libraries in order to give the programmer access to the needed methods and functions that they use to construct their code. Common functions such as array declaration can be found in the *lang* library, and mathematical operations can be found in the *math* library. This system allows programmers to pull from other people's codes, and stand on the shoulders of giants, as it were; without this system, anyone programming Java would need to write all their codes from scratch, including even the more basic functions that we take for granted.

As such, Java has the ability to reference files other than the .java text the user is probably currently already working on. It does not only have the ability to reference libraries made available by default by the Java Runtime Environment, but it can also reference other files of the more mundane kind, such as .txt files. How is this relevant? For one thing, as long as the Java library references the java.io package (which is specially designed to streamline input and output referencing by Java programs), then this makes it much easier for the programmers to access data and integrate this data with their program.

For example, a programmer wishes to write a sorting program, and he does so with an elegant algorithm. However, now that he has a sorting program, how will he make use of it? Will he have to declare each and every element he needs to sort inside his code, which defeats the purpose, and makes it useable only for that set of values? Will he create an input mechanism for the user to simply key in all the elements to be sorted? Or will he allow his sorting program to pull data from a .txt file, and immediately parse and sort through the data contained there? If your solution was the first option, then you may have a penchant for self – torture, but the second and third options require file handling, and input – output streaming.

Learning Basic File Handling

In order to begin file handling, it is important to be able to use the functions specially designed for doing so. While an immensely talented programmer may wish to build their own input / output library, most of the rest of us would probably want to use one already made specifically to deal with such tasks, and one used by almost every Java programmer out there, java.io. Accessing this library is as simple as importing the library in the first line of the .java file that you will be working on, like so:

Import java.io.*;

That command should now give the programmer access to various file handling functions such as FileInputStream, FileOutputStream, FileReader, and FileWriter.

File Input Stream

FileInputStream is one of the most basic I/O commands available in Java. This stream is used by programmers in order to read data from external files, one byte at a time. Note that the FileInputStream is a class, and as such, needs a constructor to be able to be used, like so:

```
InputStream a = new FileInputStream("C:/java/helloworld");
```

The provided constructor creates an input stream called "a", and uses it to parse and read the file helloworld contained in the *java* folder in C:. However, this is not yet enough to read it, as we only opened the stream, i.e allowed our Java program to begin to access it. What is needed, therefore, is a File object, which will place the data that we opened the stream to into a variable that can be accessed by our Java program. This can be done using the following constructor lines:

```
File a = new File("C:/java/helloworld");

InputStream a = new FileInputStream(f);
```

That will place the content of the helloworld file inside our Java program, readable through our object a, which is defined by the File class.

Now that we have the stream open and the file readable by our Java program, there are a few nifty things we can do with it. We can read from the file by using the following command:

```
public int read(int x)throws IOException{}
```

That command will allow the program to read the data of byte "x" from the input stream, and the throws IOException line will ensure that -1 will be returned if the end of the file is reached. Another command that can be used is :

```
public int available() throws IOException{}
```

Which will tell the program how many bytes can be read from this particular input stream. Closing the input stream itself, on the other hand, can be done by using the command:

```
public void close() throws IOException{}
```

Which will close the stream, and disconnect the program from further accessing the connected file.

File Output Stream

Much like its counterpart FileInputStream, the FileOutputStream function is a basic I/O command, though instead of being designed to read a particular file, it is meant to create a file and allow the Java program to write data into it. Similar to the File Input Stream, this constructor can be used to open the stream: OutputStream b = new FileOutputStream("C:/java/helloworld") which would essentially be a command to the Java program to create a stream to create .txt file named helloworld in the *java* folder located in C:.

The commands to further create an object within the Java program to be able to interact with the output stream would be similar to the File Input Stream, as follows:

```
File b = new File("C:/java/helloworld");

OutputStream b = new FileOutputStream(b);
```

Which will create the file object "b" and enable interaction between the program and the file to be written. The command of :

```
public void close() throws IOException{}
```

Which will close the stream, and disconnect the program from further accessing the connected file.

CHAPTER - 12
ADVANCED JAVA

Information Structures

The Java utility bundle gives various extremely incredible information structures that play out a scope of various capacities. These structures are comprised of the accompanying classes and interfaces:

- Enumeration

- BitSet
- Vector
- Stack
- Dictionary
- Hashtable
- Properties

The Enumeration

This interface isn't really an information structure, however it holds extraordinary significance with regards to different information structures. The interface for Enumeration characterizes a method of recovering progressive components from inside an information structure.

For instance, Enumeration characterizes something many refer to as nextElement, a technique that we use to get the following component from an information structure that has various components.

The BitSet

This class is utilized to execute a gathering of banners or bits that can be set as well as cleared on an individual premise. This is a helpful class to utilize when you should have the option to stay aware of a lot of Boolean qualities; everything you do is dole out a piece to every one of the qualities and afterward set it or clear it as required.

The Vector

This one is like the customary Java exhibit with one special case—it's ready to develop varying to oblige more components. Like the cluster, the components of the Vector object are available through a list legitimately into the Vector.

The beneficial thing about the Vector class is that there is no compelling reason to stress over setting a particular size for it when you make it—rather, it will develop and shrivel varying.

The Stack

The Stack class is liable for executing a LIFO (Last In, First Out) component stack. Think about a stack similar to a heap of articles, all piled up vertically. At the point when another one is included, it goes on head of the stack.

At the point when a component is pulled out of the stack, it also originates from the top. The keep going component to go on is the first to fall off.

The Dictionary

This is a theoretical class that characterizes an information structure for the planning of keys to esteems. This is valuable when you should have the option to get at information utilizing a particular key, rather than utilizing a number file.

Since the Dictionary class is a theoretical, it just gives you the system for an information structure that has been key-planned, instead of for a specific execution.

The Hashtable

This class gives us a methods for sorting out the information dependent on a key structure characterized by the client. For instance, on the off chance that you have a location list hashtable, you can store information and sort it dependent on a particular key, similar to a ZIP code, as opposed to utilizing names.

The significance of the keys in the hashtables is totally subject to what the hashtable is utilized for and on the information contained in it.

The Properties

This one is a subclass of the past class, hashtables, and it's utilized for keeping up arrangements of qualities. In these qualities, the key is a String, just like the worth. The Properties class is utilized by various other Java classes, i.e., it's the item type that is returned by System.getProperties() while getting natural qualities.

153

Assortments Framework

Before Java-2, Java gave us various specially appointed classes to use for the capacity and control of gatherings of items: classes, for example, Dictionary, Stack, Vector, and Properties. While these were helpful classes, they didn't have a focal subject, a bringing together topic and, thusly, the way that you utilized one of these classes was not equivalent to you would utilize another. The Collections Framework was set up to meet various significant objectives:

- It must be of elite, and the executions for the focal assortment, for example, the dynamic cluster, trees, connected records, and hashtables, are exceptionally proficient.
- The system expected to let various sorts of assortments work in a way that was like one another and to have the option to interoperate to a serious extent.
- It must be anything but difficult to broaden and additionally adjust an assortment.

To this end, the system has been structured around a lot of interfaces that have been normalized. There are various standard usage of the interfaces that can be utilized as they seem to be, and you can likewise execute an assortment based on your very own preference. A portion of the standard usage are HashSet, LinkedList, and TreeSet.

An assortment structure is a design that has been bound together for the portrayal and control of assortments. Each structure has the accompanying:

- Interfaces: These are theoretical information types that are illustrative of assortments. They permit every one of the assortments to be autonomously controlled, outside of the subtleties of portrayals. In any article arranged language, interfaces will as a rule structure a progression.
- Implementations, i.e., Classes: These are strong usage of every one of the assortment interfaces; they are fundamentally information structures that can be reused.
- Algorithms: Algorithms are strategies utilized for performing helpful calculations, such as looking and arranging, on any item that may execute an assortment interface. These calculations are supposed to be "polymorphic," which implies that one strategy can be utilized on various usage of a fitting assortment interface.

Just as assortments, the Framework likewise characterizes various classes and guide interfaces. Guides are utilized to store key and worth sets and, despite the fact that they are not assortments thusly, they are coordinated with them.

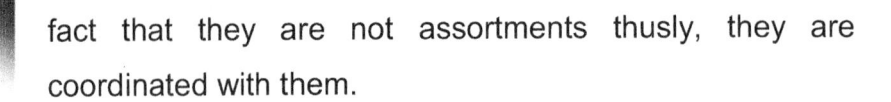

The Collection Interfaces

Various interfaces are characterized by the assortments structure. The table underneath gives you a short clarification of every interface:

Interfaces with Description

The Collection Interface

This permits you to work with object gatherings and is at the head of the chain of importance.

The List Interface

This expands the Collection interface and a case of this one stores an assortment of components that are requested.

The Set

This one expands Collection so it can deal with sets. These sets need to contain components that are special.

The SortedSet

This will broaden Set with the goal that it can deal with arranged sets.

The Map

This guides one of a kind keys to values.

The Map.Entry

This depicts a component, or a key/esteem pair, in a guide and is an inward class of Map.

The SortedMap

This stretches out Map so as to permit the keys to be kept up in a climbing request.

The Enumeration

This is a heritage interface that characterizes techniques that you can use to list or get each in turn, components from an assortment of articles. This has now been supplanted by Iterator.

The Collection Classes

Just as the assortment interfaces, Java additionally gives us various standard assortment classes, which are all intended to execute the interfaces somewhat or other. Some will give a full usage that can be utilized as they seem to be, and others are a greater amount of a theoretical class, a weakened execution that is utilized absolutely as a beginning stage for making increasingly strong assortments. The accompanying table is a synopsis of the standard assortment classes.

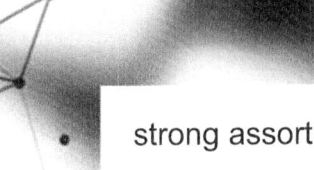

Classes with Description

AbstractCollection

Executes practically the entirety of the assortment interface.

AbstractList

Executes the greater part of the List interface and furthermore broadens AbstractCollection.

AbstractSequential

Broadens AbstractList so an assortment that utilizes successive component get to, as opposed to arbitrary access, can utilize it.

LinkedList

Stretches out AbstractSequentialList to actualize a connected rundown.

ArrayList

Expands AbstractList with the goal that a unique exhibit can be actualized.

AbstractSet

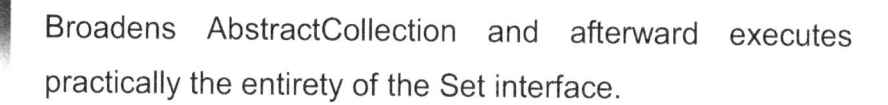

Broadens AbstractCollection and afterward executes practically the entirety of the Set interface.

HashSet

Broadens AbstractSet so it very well may be utilized with a hashtable.

LinkedHashSet

Broadens HashSet with the goal that inclusion request cycles can be utilized.

TreeSet

Expands AbstractSet and furthermore permits usage of sets that are put away in trees.

AbstractMap

Actualizes practically the entirety of the Map interface.

HashMap

Expands AbstractMap so it can utilize a hashtable.

TreeMap

Expands AbstractMap so it can utilize a tree.

WeakHashMap

Expands AbstractMap so it can utilize a hashtable that contains powerless keys.

LinkedHashMap

Expands HashMap with the goal that addition request collaborations can be utilized.

IdentityHashMap

Expands AbstractMap and will likewise utilize reference equity when it thinks about reports.

The accompanying classes just give an essential, skeletal usage of center interfaces with the goal that the exertion expected to execute them is diminished:

- AbstractCollection
- AbstractSet
- AbstractList
- AbstractMap
- AbstractSequentialList

The Collection Algorithms

The assortments system likewise characterizes various calculations that might be applied to specific guides and assortments. These are characterized inside the Collections class as static strategies.

A portion of these techniques can toss a ClassCastException. This happens when an endeavor is made to look at incongruent kinds. These strategies likewise hurl an UnsupportedOperationException when an endeavor is made to change an assortment that can't be adjusted.

CHAPTER - 13
MODULES

The Java module, also known as Project Jigsaw, is a collection of packages. It is one of the highlight features that were introduced with the release of Java 9. This particular program underwent development and piloting for several years before it was finally included in the Java 9 release. The program was slated for launch with Java 7 and later with Java 8, but failed on both occasions due to unknown reasons in the public domain that led to the delays. The Java module has since become a crucial aspect of software development.

A Java module facilitates the bundling of applications and packages in a way that controls the functionality of the packages. As such, a Java module is created when the applications and packages are transformed into a single suit. The Java module moderates the visibility of its packages to other Java modules. This way, the Java module is able to determine the packages that can be accessed or reused by other modules on the one hand, and the specific modules it must interact with to complete tasks on the other. The program achieves the controlled distribution through the segmentation of packages into either exported or concealed categories. Exported packages are readily exposed to access and interaction with other packages within a module. Concealed packages are restricted to the internal coding operations of the module and cannot interact with external packages.

Advantages of Java Modules

The Java module provides significant advantages for Java programmers. For example, the feature was introduced to enhance efficiency in the reuse of classes and save Java programmers the efforts of writing new codes. The inheritance properties and interface capabilities are the crucial elements that facilitate the reuse of classes and objects.

Fragmentation of the Java modules into autonomous units makes it easier for developers to determine and select the preferred specifications for applications. This helps decongest the Java development environment because developers have the flexibility to limit selections to the modules that are required for particular applications. This is a departure from the pre-Java 9 versions that lumped many APIs and applications together because they lacked mechanisms for predicting the classes that would be required in the programming processes. The increased use of Java in small or handheld devices like mobile phones and tablets has necessitated the development of light-weight and fragmented solutions, such as the Java module, for packaging applications.

Missing Java modules trigger error warnings during startup. In fact, the JVM cannot launch operations if it detects missing modules. This allows developers to make corrections well in advance as opposed to experiencing the inconvenience of unexpected module gaps during runtime. Late discovery of a missing module may prompt a developer to abandon a work-in-progress and start an application development process all over again. This was mostly the case in the pre-Java 9 series.

Objectives of Java Modules

The modularization of Java 9 was informed by various objectives that included the consolidation of configuration parameters, strengthening of encapsulation, condensation of Java's scalability and integrity, and the enhancement of performance. All these factors contributed to the elevation of the modular programs to a higher level that packages because of the greater functionalities that they introduced to Java programming.

Configuration upgrades through the modularity solution were needed to implement dependency declarations that were capable of hastening compilation and execution processes. Strengthened encapsulation simplified the management of packages and their relationship to the modules with respect to managing data accessibility within programs. There was an urgent need for a solution that was capable of supporting explicit declarations of the capabilities that were required to facilitate interactions between different modules. The limitations imposed on the minimum interaction requirements are useful in enhancing the security of the Java platform.

The scaling aspect organized the formerly scattered Java programs and tools into a specific number of modules that can be identified with ease. The scaled properties of the modules provide greater flexibility for customizing the scope of module utilization. The platform integrity objective eliminated the deployment of unnecessary apps during application development processes. Modularization streamlined app deployment through the introduction of encapsulation mechanisms for concealing the classes. Enhanced performance was definitely the overall objective of the modularization transformation. The Java 9 modules provide predictive tools for determining the exact modules needed for particular programming activities, and this allows the JVM to operate more efficiently.

Insights into the Structure of Java 9 Module

According to Deitel (n.d.), the Java module was initially launched as Project Jigsaw, but was later renamed and modularized into Java 9 where it sits on top of packages. This module requires developers to observe certain conditions when building applications using Java 9. For example, a unique naming system is used in addition to the provision of specific descriptions of its dependencies.

A Java module consists of a directory structure, a declarator, and a source code. The three items actually form the sequence for creating a Java module. There are specifications for creating a directory structure and declaring the module, but the specifications of the directory structure are not significantly different from the specifications that are applied in the creation of Java packages. However, it is important to remember that a module and the sources of the module bear a similar name that is modeled on a reverse domain pattern. For example, a Sample Coding preferred unique name of the module would appear as: com.samplecoding.

The declarator hosts the metadata definitions of the dependencies of a module alongside the packages that the module is capable of extending to other modules. It actually exists as the compiled format of a module declaration as per the definitions contained in the module-info.java file. The keyword 'module' appears as the compulsory first word in a declaration.

A unique name that follows the module facilitates its identification from other modules. An ideal descriptor name would appear as follows: *module modulename*, followed by an opening curly brace at the end of the name and a closing curly brace that is aligned to the left below the name. If we use the Sample Coding name as the unique identification of the module, the descriptor name would appear as follows:

```
module com.samplecoding{

}
```

The body of the declaration is positioned between the two curly braces, but the body segment is optional as you may choose to leave it empty or include commands for performing specific operations such as *exports*, *opens*, *provides*, and *requires*. The other widely used commands include: *uses*, *to*, and *with*. As such, a module name and opening and closing curly braces are sufficient to a construct a declarator. The module creation process involves several steps that require you to construct a directory structure, declarator, and a source code.

- Step one: We will follow the widely practiced format and use the src as the root directory for our source files. Create the src directory, label it with the unique name of the module, and save. In this particular example, the src is the equivalent of the uniquely named module file — that is, com.samplecoding. But you still need to create the com.samplecoding folder and save it in the src folder to comply with the recommended module structure.
- Step two: Create a module-info.java text editor file and execute an empty module declaration within that file. Remember that the name of the declared module should be similar to the name of the directory that houses it. In this example, this step simply involves making the com.samplecoding declaration inside a

module-info.java program file, and saving it in the src folder.

```
module-info.java - Notepad
module com.samplecoding{
}
```

- Step three: In the com.samplecoding, split the reverse domain from the module name and use each of the two parts to create two folders. Start with the com folder and store it in the com.samplecoding folder. Proceed to create a samplecoding folder and store it in the com folder. At this point the module structure has transformed as follows: the src folder contains the com.samplecoding folder, which in turn houses the com folder and the module-info.java file. The com folder contains the samplecoding folder, which in turn will store a source code of the Java program to be compiled in the next step.
- Step four: Open a new text editor and construct a source code of your choice. This example is using SampleItem and SampleItem.java as the class and file name, respectively. Save the program file in the samplecoding folder with the SampleItem.java name, while the rest of the files will maintain their names and positions in the directory structure.

```
public class SampleItem{

public static void main(String[] args){

System.out.println("Sample item for testing Java module");

}

}
```

- Step five: Compile the module in javac to create a class file. The compilation process involves the use of a command. For this particular example, the command would read as follows: javac –d mods --module-source-path src/ --module com.samplecoding. This converts the module-info.java and SampleItem.java files into module-info.class and SampleItem.class, respectively. The compilation procedure will also replace the src with mods as the root directory.

Exercise

Steps one to three provide a detailed description of a module structure. Use the description to create a diagram of the module structure.

Solution:

```
            src
          com.samplecoding
module-info.java           com
                        samplecoding
                        SampleItem.java
```

Summary

- The Java module was initially unveiled as Project Jigsaw and was introduced alongside Java 9.
- The Java module contains a variety of packages that allow developers to determine and control the functionality of Java programs.
- A Java module is labeled using a unique naming system and specific descriptions of its dependencies.

CHAPTER - 14
PROJECTS

Hello World

Traditionally, everyone's first program prints "Hello World". This first program demonstrates how to create, save, and run a program. It also shows the basic structure used in all Java programs.

Here's a screenshot of the window created by the Hello World program:

Do-It-Yourself Java Games
File Edit Size
Hello World

Lesson 1.1 - Java Projects and Packages

Programs are first organized by Java projects, then by packages within the Java projects. You'll create a Java project for each program.

Packages hold program files that are usually used together. Because the programs will be small, most of the Java projects you create will have only one package.

In this lesson, you'll create one Java project and one package for your first program.

Try It

Create your first Java project, called *Hello World:*

1. If Eclipse is no longer open:
   a. Double-click the *Eclipse* shortcut you created on your desktop.

b. Click *OK* to use your Java work folder as your workspace.

2. Right-click in the *Package Explorer* pane and choose *New / Java Project*.

3. Name the Java project *Hello World*, and select *Use Default JRE* if it is 1.7 or higher, then click *Next* as shown in the image below. If the default JRE is less than 1.7, select the option to *Use an execution environment JRE* of 1.7 or higher.

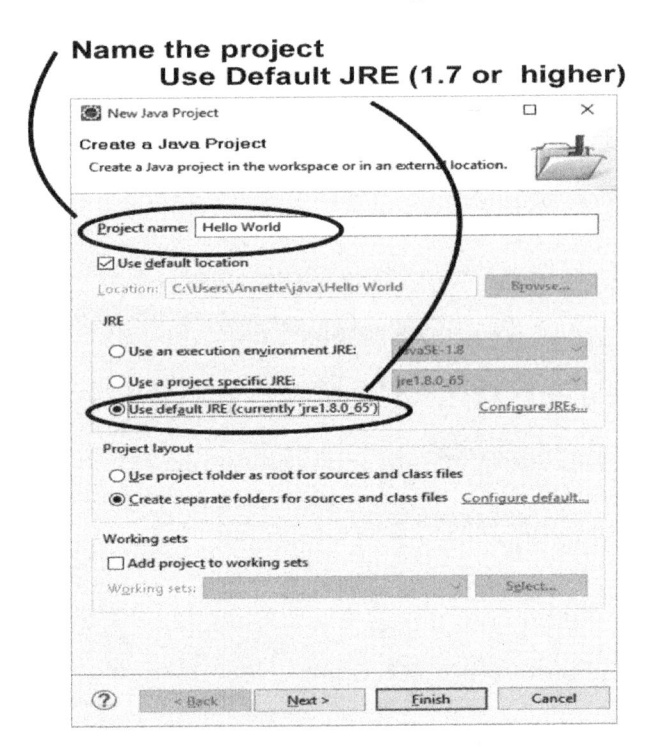

4. Click *Libraries*, then click *Add External JARs...*, as shown in the image below.

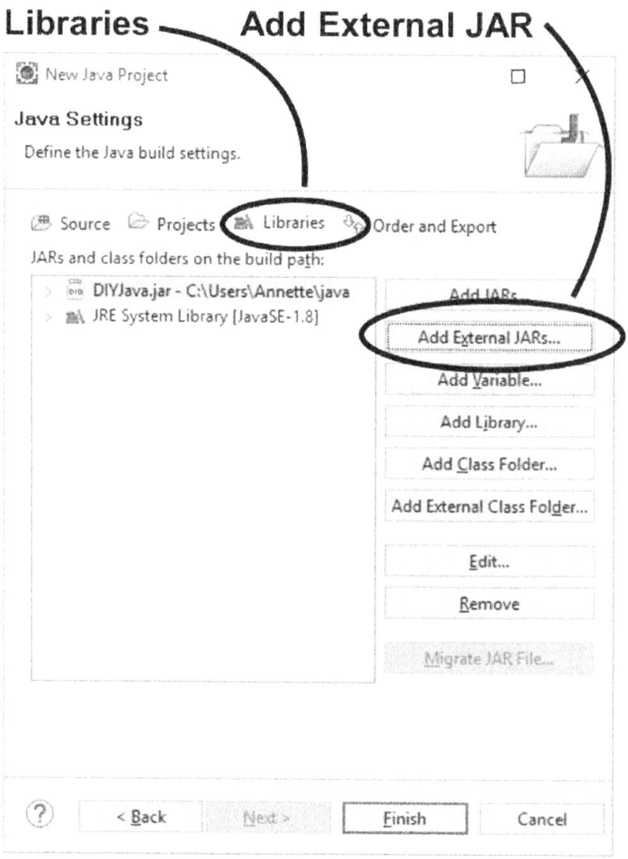
Libraries
Add External JAR
New Java Project
Java Settings
Define the Java build settings.
Source
Projects
Libraries
Order and Export
JARs and class folders on the build path:
DIYJava.jar - C:\Users\Annette\java
JRE System Library [JavaSE-1.8]
Add JARs...
Add External JARs...
Add Variable...
Add Library...
Add Class Folder...
Add External Class Folder...
Edit...
Remove
Migrate JAR File...
< Back
Next >
Finish
Cancel

5. Browse to and select *DIYJava.jar*, which you installed in your Java work folder, and click *Open*.

6. Click *Finish*.

The *Package Explorer* pane now lists one project (*Hello World*) with the added JAR file (*DIYJava.jar*), as shown in this image:

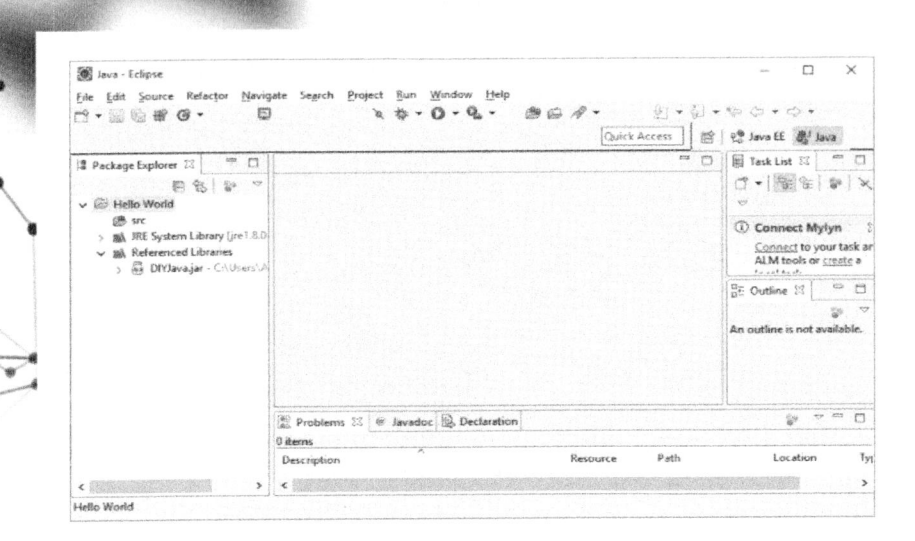

Create a package for your Hello World program in the *Hello World* project:

1. Right-click on the *Hello World* project and choose *New / Package*.

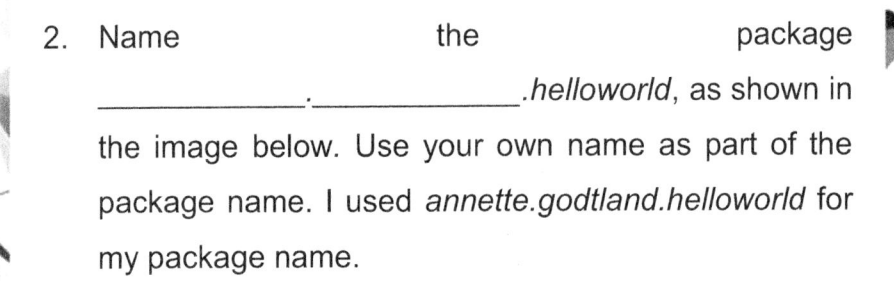

2. Name the package _____._____.*helloworld*, as shown in the image below. Use your own name as part of the package name. I used *annette.godtland.helloworld* for my package name.

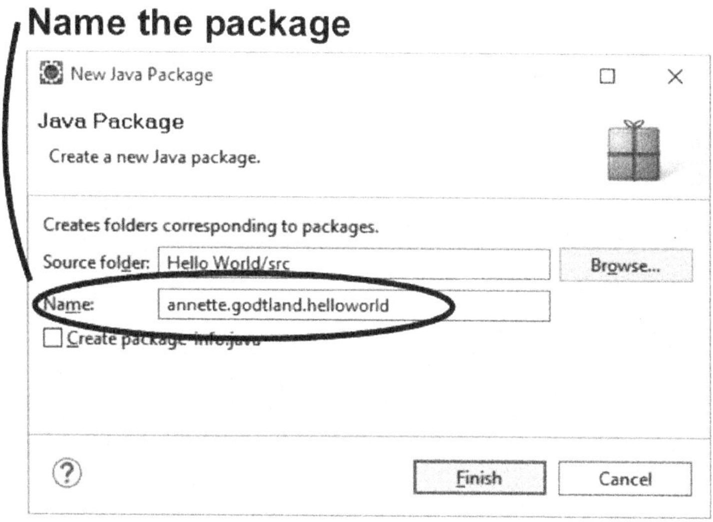
Name the package
New Java Package
Java Package
Create a new Java package.
Creates folders corresponding to packages.
Source folder: Hello World/src
Browse...
Name: annette.godtland.helloworld
Create package-info.java
Finish
Cancel

3. Click *Finish*.

The *Package Explorer* pane now shows the package you created in your *Hello World* project, as shown in this image:

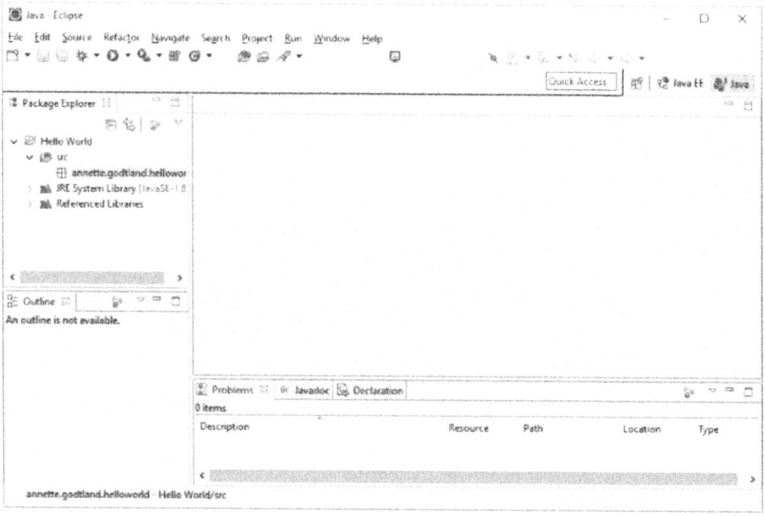
Java - Eclipse
File Edit Source Refactor Navigate Search Project Run Window Help
Quick Access
Java EE
Java
Package Explorer
Hello World
src
annette.godtland.hellowor
JRE System Library
Referenced Libraries
Outline
An outline is not available.
Problems
Javadoc
Declaration
0 items
Description
Resource
Path
Location
Type
annette.godtland.helloworld - Hello World/src

Key Points and More

- Right-click in the *Package Explorer* pane to create Java projects and packages.
- Create a different Java project for each program.
- Eclipse will create a folder on your computer named the same as the Java project. Give your Java project a name you want for the folder on your computer.
    - You now have a folder called *Hello World* in your Java work folder.
    - For example, capitalize the first letter of each word and put a space between each word like the *Hello World* project.
- Add *DIYJava.jar* to the Java projects you create with the help of this book.
    - *DIYJava.jar* is an external JAR file.
    - *DIYJava.jar* makes it easy to write programs that print text to a window.
- Organize your program files into packages in Java projects.
- Put program files that are usually used together into one package.
    - Because your programs will be small, most of your programs will have only one package.
- Package name rules:

- Make your package name different from anyone else's package names. Java programmers traditionally use their name or business name as the first part of their package name.
- Use all lowercase letters with no spaces.
- Use periods between different categories in the package name. For example, if the package name identifies who created the package and what the package will be used for, put a period between the creator and its purpose.
* Make sure when you create the Java Projects, you should select the option to *Use an execution environment JRE of JavaSE-1.7* or higher. Once you select this option for creating a project, Eclipse will default to that option for all future Java Projects.
* Java projects are for Eclipse; packages are for Java. Because you're using Eclipse, you'll use both Java projects and packages. If you were to create Java programs without Eclipse, you would probably use only packages.

Lesson 1.2 - Classes, Superclasses and Programs

Java programs are made from one or more classes. Classes contain the actual program code: the instructions that, when run in sequence, perform a desired task.

Every class must name some other class as its superclass. For example, programs intended to run in a window must name some type of window class as its superclass.

In this lesson, you'll create your first class: a program that runs in a *DIYWindow*.

Try It

Create your first class using the *DIYWindow* class as its superclass:

1. Right-click on your package in the *Package Explorer* pane and choose *New / Class*.

2. Enter *HelloWorld* for the class name, as shown in the image below. (Hint: there's no space between "Hello" and "World".)

3. Click *Browse* for *Superclass*.

4. Enter "diy" for the *type*, select *DIYWindow,* as shown in the image below, and click *OK*.

Name the class

Browse to and select Superclass DIYWindow

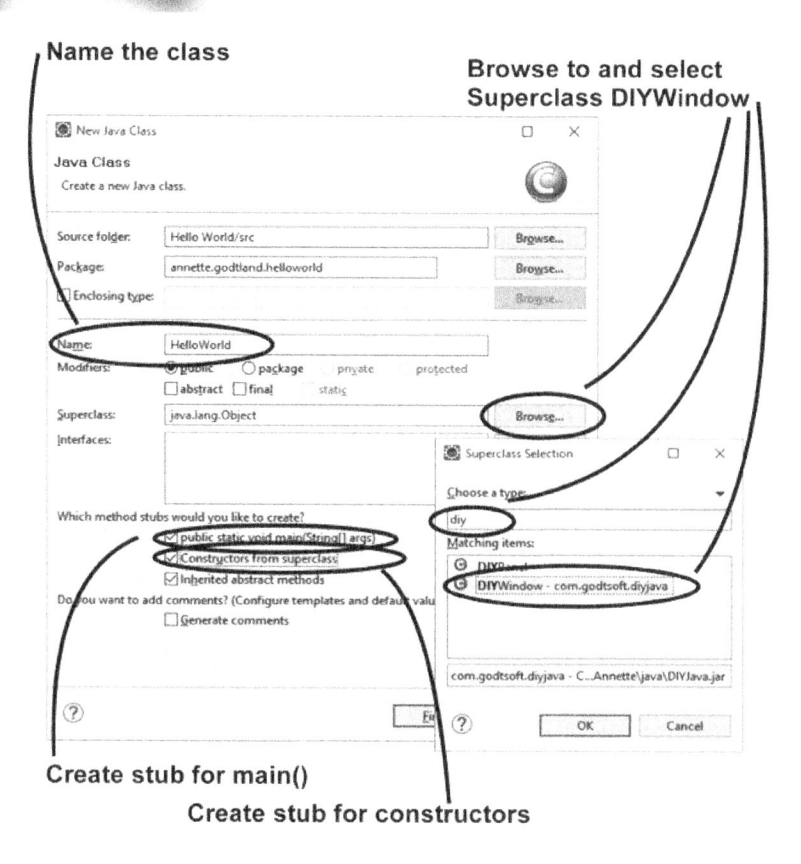

Create stub for main()

Create stub for constructors

5. Click *Finish* to create the class.

Eclipse will create code for a *HelloWorld* class that looks like the following listing.

You may find it easier to read the code listings, if you set your e-reader to a smaller font to minimize word wrapping.

Listing 1-1, from HelloWorld.java

```
package annette.godtland.helloworld;
import com.godtsoft.diyjava.DIYWindow;
public class HelloWorld extends DIYWindow {
```

```
public HelloWorld() {
    // TODO Auto-generated constructor stub
}
public static void main(String[] args) {
    // TODO Auto-generated method stub
}
}
```

Completed listing

Eclipse adds comment code you don't need. Comments are lines that begin with // or groups of lines that begin with /* and end with */.

1. Remove the automatically-generated comment lines from this class, where it says *(Code was removed from here.)* in the following listing.

Listing 1-2, from HelloWorld.java

```
package annette.godtland.helloworld;
import com.godtsoft.diyjava.DIYWindow;
public class HelloWorld extends DIYWindow {
    public HelloWorld() {
```
(Code was removed from here.)
```
    }
    public static void main(String[] args) {
```
(Code was removed from here.)

```
    }
}
```

- Completed listing

Click any *Completed listing* link to see how to complete the code. However, you'll learn more if you try to complete the code yourself before you look up the answer.

The block of code that starts as *public static void main* is called the *main()* method. The block of code that starts as *public HelloWorld()* is called the constructor.

Now, add your first lines of code:

1. Add code to the constructor and *main()* method exactly as shown here. Changes to make to code are always shown bold in the listings.

Listing 1-3, from HelloWorld.java

```
package annette.godtland.helloworld;

import com.godtsoft.diyjava.DIYWindow;

public class HelloWorld extends DIYWindow {

    public HelloWorld() {
```

```
    print("Hello World");
  }
  public static void main(String[] args) {
    new HelloWorld();
  }
}
```

Completed listing

1. Press *Ctrl-S* to save the program.

2. Click the *Run* button, as shown in this image, to run the program:

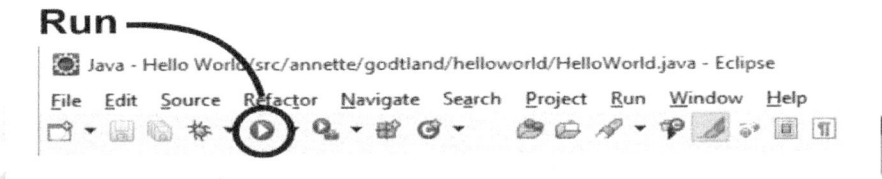

What happened?

A window should open that displays "Hello World", as shown in this image:

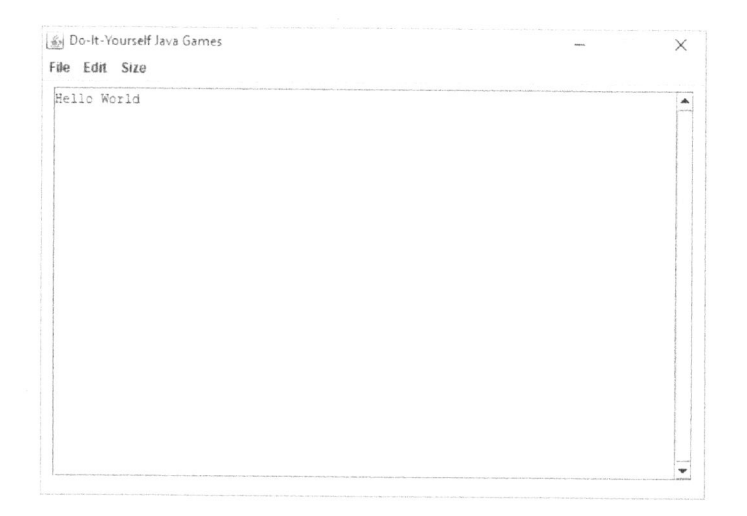

```
Do-It-Yourself Java Games            —    ×
File  Edit  Size
Hello World
```

1. What would you have to change in your class to make it say hello to *you*?

Listing 1-4, from HelloWorld.java

...

public HelloWorld() {
  print("Hello _____ ");
}

...

Completed listing

1. Save the program and run it.

What happens if you make a mistake?

1. Type the word "print" incorrectly and save the program.

Listing 1-5, from HelloWorld.java

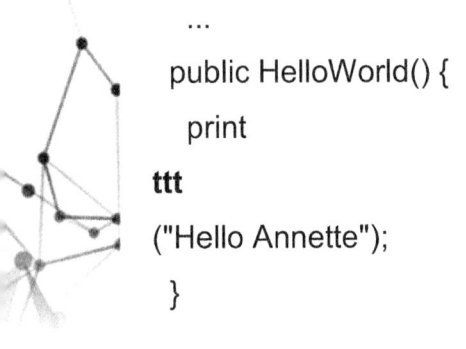

...

public HelloWorld() {

print

ttt

("Hello Annette");

}

...

Completed listing

What happened?

Many error indicators appear, as shown in this image:

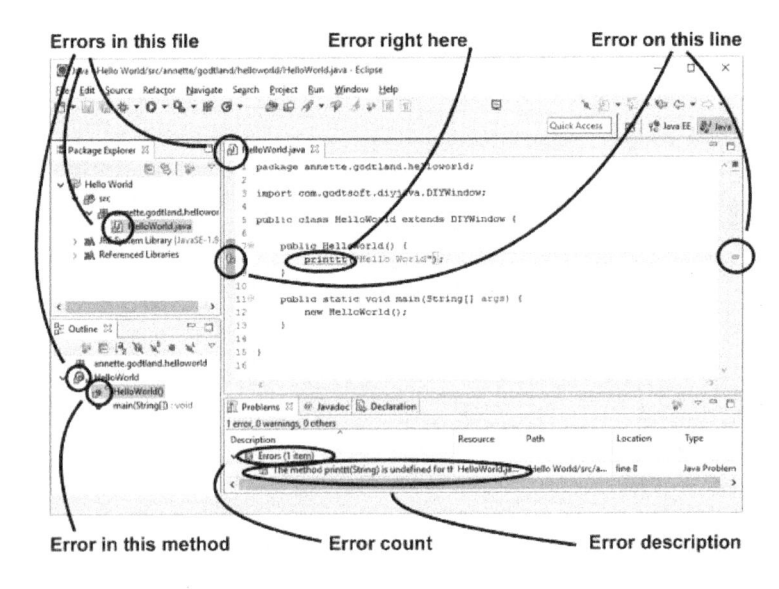

- Errors in this file
- Error right here
- Error on this line
- Error in this method
- Error count
- Error description

1. Double-click the Error count in the *Problems* pane of Eclipse to see the list of errors found.

2. Double-click on the Error description in the *Problems* pane to move your cursor to the line with the error.

3. Rest your cursor on the actual error (where it says *Error right here* in the above image). Eclipse will list ways to fix the problem, as shown in the image below. This feature of Eclipse is called *Quick Fix*.

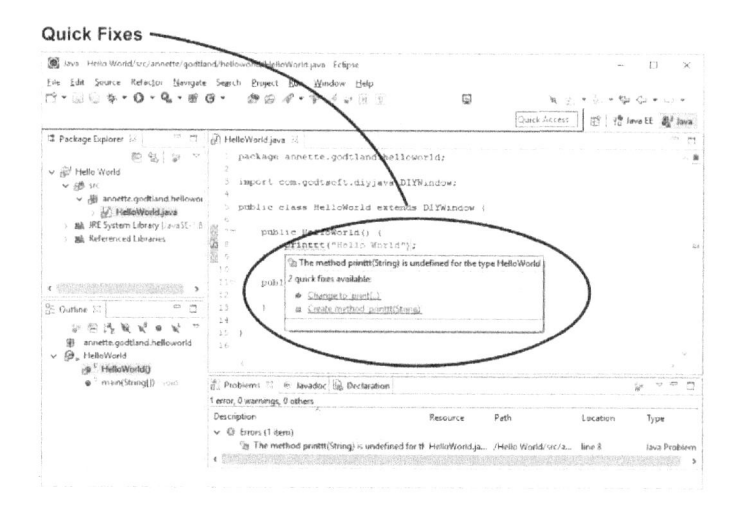

4. Click the quick fix called *Change to "print(...)"*.

That action will fix the error for you.

1. Save changes.

All error indicators should disappear.

Now, print more:

1. Change the code to make your program say this:

Hello, earthling.

Take me to your leader.

Listing 1-6, from HelloWorld.java

...

```
public HelloWorld() {
    print("_____");

    print("_____");

}
```

...

Completed listing

Throughout the lessons, unless there are <u>syntax errors</u>, save changes and run the program after every code change.

Did it print the correct lines? If not, fix the code and try again.

1. What do you think you would have to print to put a blank line between the two sentences, as shown below. (Hint: you want nothing printed on that line.)

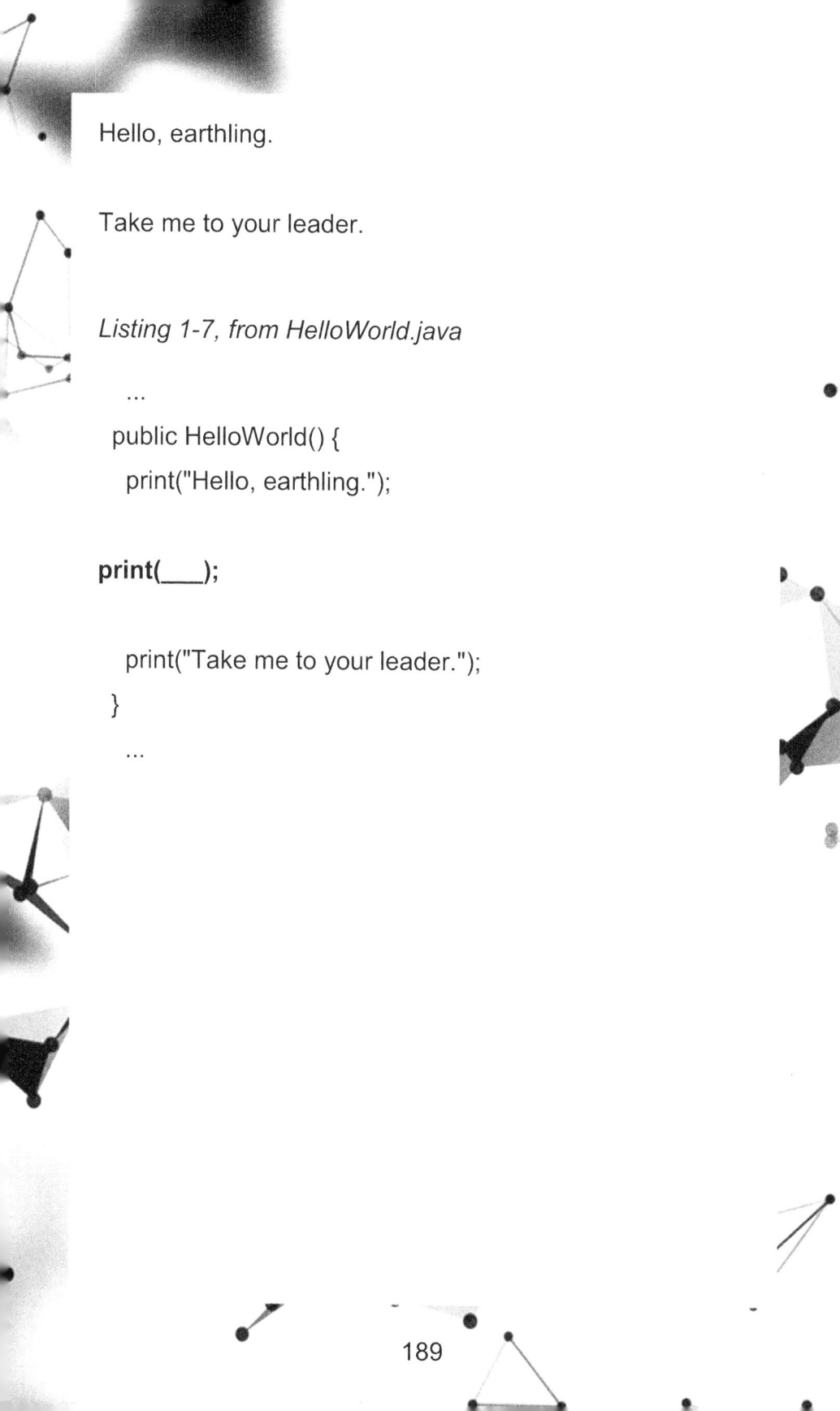

Hello, earthling.

Take me to your leader.

Listing 1-7, from HelloWorld.java

```
...
  public HelloWorld() {
    print("Hello, earthling.");
```

print(___);

```
    print("Take me to your leader.");
  }
...
```

CONCLUSION

This book provides useful information on the basics of Java programming. However, Java is a very broad field of study, and a single book may not be enough to cover all areas on this particular topic. Once you are familiar with the basics of Java programming, you should expand your knowledge by exploring the programming language at the intermediate and advanced levels. Therefore, the parts in this book are designed to prepare you for the most challenging and adventurous application of Java programming. This book will always remain your important reference partner, even as you progress through the intermediate and advanced levels of the programming language.

Java is a valuable programming language with a wide variety of uses. It is practical, effective and extremely easy to use. It will be a great asset and benchmark for your planning future. If you can think about it, you can create it. Don't be afraid to try something new.

Java is a very powerful language, it dominates most companies and organizations. It is one of the best languages for developers when they want to implement web based applications. Also, software devices that need to communicate with each other over a given network are developed with the help of Java. Many devices today use Java. To become a great Java programmer, you must take the time to read in depth and learn the concepts in Java. Fortunately, this book helps you develop the right knowledge to expand further in other areas of Java. Therefore, the next step after reading this book is to find a complete Java manual to read.

Java is a very broad field of study, and a single book may not be enough to cover all areas on this particular topic. Once you are familiar with the basics of Java programming, you should expand your knowledge by exploring the programming language at the intermediate and advanced levels. Therefore, the parts in this book are designed to prepare you for the most challenging and adventurous application of Java programming. This book will always remain your important reference partner, even as you progress through the intermediate and advanced levels of the programming language.

There are plenty of other coding languages that you can work with, but Java is one of the best that works for most novice developers as it provides the power and ease of use that you are looking for when you first start in this type.

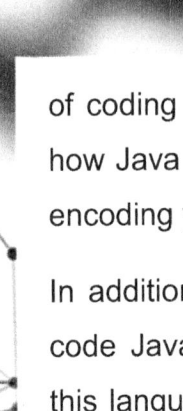

of coding language. . This guide took the time to explore how Java works, along with some of the different types of encoding you can do with it.

In addition to looking at many examples of how you can code Java and how to create some of your programs in this language, we also spent time discussing how to work with Java when it comes to the world of machine learning, artificial intelligence, and data analytics. These are problems and parts of technology that are taking off and many developers are trying to learn more about it. And with the help of this guide, you will be able to handle all of this, even as a Java beginner.

When you're ready to learn more about working with the Java coding language and how to make sure you can even use Java in conjunction with data analytics, artificial intelligence, and machine learning, be sure to check this guide again to help you get started.

Printed in Great Britain
by Amazon